Light the FIRE

Raising Up a Generation to Live Radically for Jesus Christ

Alvin L. Reid

WINEPRESS WP PUBLISHING

Printed in the United States of America.

Packaged by WinePress Publishing, PO Box 428, Enumclaw, WA 98022. The views expressed or implied in this work do not necessarily reflect those of WinePress Publishing. Ultimate design, content, and editorial accuracy of this work is the responsibility of the author.

Unless otherwise noted all scriptures are taken from the New King James Version, Copyright © 1979, 1980, 1982 by Thomas Nelson, Inc., Publishers. Used by permission.

ISBN 1-57921-341-3
Library of Congress Catalog Card Number: 00-110230

Dedication

To Brad Jurkovich,
one of the finest young evangelists in America,
for your encouragement in this project and for your
ministry to the
youth of America.

Contact Brad Jurkovich's
Be the Light Ministry at
www.bethelight.org

Also to the team of students who travel with me:
Lori Calloway, Matt Blaxton, Trent Eayrs, Andy Ehlers,
April Johnson, Jenny Justice, and Jill Lengel.
God has used you to fuel my passion for youth.

Finally, to the coming generation of young people who I
believe will
change the whole world.

── Acknowledgments

MANY HAVE ENCOURAGED ME IN THE WRITING OF THIS BOOK. FIRST, I give glory to the Lord Jesus Christ for instilling a passion in me from my youth to see Him work in great revival, especially among young people. After the Lord, no one is more precious than my wife of almost 20 years, Michelle, and the greatest kids on earth, Josh and Hannah. Thanks for your patience with my hours on the laptop, gang!

Brad Jurkovich, one of the finest young evangelists in America, has been the primary catalyst for this project. His encouragement has made him a Barnabas to me. May God raise up a thousand like him! Brad also helped with some of the research for the book. Matt Queen, Lori Calloway, Jonathan Adams, Larry McDonald, Andy Ehlers, and others read some or all of the manuscript and gave great advice. Laura Fuller, my secretary, helped bunches with the final typing and printing.

Richard Ross, perhaps the most influential leader of youth ministers in America, has become a Jonathan to this David in recent years. His influence goes far beyond the wonderful Foreword he wrote for this book. Thanks Richard!

Most of all, I thank God for the thousands of incredible teenagers I have met over the past several years. Your passion feeds my flame for God. May God allow you to see mighty revival in your generation.

Foreword

—Richard Ross

A FEW YEARS AGO I BEGAN TO NOTICE A CHANGE IN THE ATTITUDE and passion of students. This growing passion, seen first in students under sixteen, but now obvious in youth from middle school through college, is a demonstration of the activity of God in our day. Perhaps our great God is preparing a fresh generation for a great movement of His Spirit!

The movement God has honored called True Love Waits is dear to my heart. Only He could have made it as influential as it has been as tens of thousands of students have committed to purity. I once thought that the campaign of asking students to pledge sexual abstinence before marriage was an end in itself in order to bring glory to God and to avoid the human tragedies that always accompany immorality. However, I now can see that the purity movement is but one of several streams of revival. Just look at the other signs of God's activity among youth in the past few years—See You at the Pole, the rapid rise of Christian clubs, and the courage of Christian youth in recent national tragedies, to name only a few. And these are only a larger, more visible picture of what God has begun to do in youth rallies, in student groups, and in church youth groups on a smaller but very widespread scale beneath the surface. If sovereign God so wills, those separate streams may soon join in a wonderful, majestic confluence of spiritual energy.

Throughout history, as revival begins to spread, God uses the retelling of the stories of revival to spread the fires. If we believe students may very well lead the next movement of God, why on earth would we limit the re-telling of stories to adults? Alvin Reid is right on time with his conviction that students will be even more bold when they read the stories of what God has done through their generation down through history.

This book can in fact "light the fire" in the hearts of students to live lives radically sold out to Jesus. God is calling youth to a new level of devotion, in personal devotion, in missions service, in roles of leadership, in reaching this lost culture. Get this book in the hands of your students–and their parents, and student ministers, and pastors for that matter–and see what God can do!

Richard Ross
Fort Worth, Texas
October, 2000

——Light the Fire Again

I stand to praise You
But I fall on my knees
My spirit is willing
But my flesh is so weak

Chorus:
So light the Fire in my soul
Fan the flame make me whole
Lord you know where I've been
So light the fire in my heart again

I feel Your arms around me
As the power of Your healing begins
Your Spirit rushes through me
Like a Mighty rushing wind

So light the Fire in my soul
Fan the flame make me whole
Lord you know where I've been
So light the fire in my heart again[1]

Contents

———————— Introduction

I HAVE A PROBLEM WITH HURRICANES. WELL, NOT JUST ANY HURRI-
canes, but hurricanes with names that begin with "F." Hurricane Fran smashed my beautiful Gran Prix with a big pine
tree in 1996. Then, in 1999, hurricane Floyd pushed a tree
over on top of our house. East of us, dozens died, and thousands lost their homes, because of Floyd's fury.

On September 15, 1999, my family watched CNN to
track the path of Floyd as it moved inland from the coast at
Wilmington. Suddenly, the program was interrupted with
the news of a church shooting in Fort Worth. We were in
shock. Our shock turned to horror when the name of the
church was given—Wedgwood Baptist Church. Michelle
and I were members there in the 1980s while I attended
Southwestern Seminary. The same youth group I once

worked with was now victimized by a madman. Worse than that, the gunman attacked during a See You at the Pole student rally. As young people gathered to sing praises to God and pray for revival, Larry Gene Ashbrook desecrated their devotion with his rampage.

This tragedy illustrates in a stark way how badly we need God to sweep across our nation in great revival. True revival comes when the Spirit of God moves Christians to radical obedience. Revival equals *radical* Christianity—not the ho-hum, show-up-at-church-and-leave-unchanged kind, but the kind where you live consumed by the thought of honoring God and changing your world! Did you know that revivals often touch young people more powerfully than adults? And, most movements of God in the past have started with students.[2] Did you know, for example, that what historians called the First Great Awakening in the American colonies began in no small part because of the response of Christian young people? Or, that students on college campuses played a pivotal role in a great revival about two hundred years ago in the United States? Well, more of that later, but my point is this: there is just something about the passion of youth that is contagious, and God can use that passion to touch a nation.

Just imagine for a minute—what if you and your friends in middle school, high school, or college were about to experience a fresh touch from God? What if God were getting ready to rock the nation with a spiritual awakening? It has happened before. Charles Finney, a man who saw God radically change tens of thousands in a great revival called the Second Great Awakening, observed that God often sends revival after a time of moral and spiritual decline. We must be ripe for revival then! Right now, as you read this, God *is* stirring many teenagers from California to the Carolinas. Do you want Him to use you greatly? Then read on.

I am not a prophet. I cannot say for sure whether we are on the verge of a great revival. Two things are clear. First, we desperately need revival in our land. Second, God seems to be raising up a new generation, one more ripe for revival than in decades. God has spread the flame of revival on numerous occasions in the past, and young people have provided the best fuel for His glory. Will you allow God to use *you* to fulfil His purposes? Will you let God light the fire in your heart?

Chapter One

Vision

Let no one despise your youth,
but be an example to the believers in word,
in conduct, in love, in spirit, in faith, in purity.

I Timothy 4:12

God does not bless great talent,
He blesses great likeness to Jesus.

—Robert Murray McCheyne

Rachel Scott.
Cassie Bernall.
Jeremiah Neitz.

IF SOMEONE ASKED YOU IN JANUARY OF 1999 TO NAME THE PEOPLE
you would choose as the most significant Christians in
America for that year, these are probably not the ones you
would have chosen. In fact, you may not recognize these
names now. But God knows who they are. Bernall and Scott
died for their faith at Columbine High School in Littleton,

Colorado. Neitz stood boldly in the face of an attacker at Wedgwood Baptist Church.

America has changed. Shootings in schools and random violence have become a common occurrence. Now we have Christian martyrs, people who died for their faith. Right here in America. More significantly, the dead are all young.

Make no mistake, it is still far safer to be a Christian in America than in most places of the world. Try living for Jesus in Saudi Arabia or Somalia, for example. You are more likely to die young in an automobile accident than to die as a martyr. The point I am trying to make is that God seems to be raising up people, *young* people, who are willing to abandon everything to Jesus. It is not only that some students are taking the bullets. Students are making a difference in culture—in schools, in local churches, and in homes across America.

God appears to be raising up a new generation of students. You are part of a movement much bigger than your local school or church. This book is a challenge for you to live a life abandoned to God.

Think of it this way—at the Olympics, many of the athletes who compete for and win gold medals are in their teens. If a student your age can compete in the Olympics, a student like you can be a champion for Jesus!

What a Time to Be Alive!

We are only the second generation of people who have lived on this earth to experience a new millennium since our Lord walked through Palestine. This is a unique time. It is also a dangerous time.

Every generation of youth faces challenges, but in the world today, the extremes are greater, and the stakes are higher. In my high school days in the 70s, we had fire drills

A recent survey showed that teen violence is a serious issue in our society:

- 27% of teens were involved in a physical attack on another person
- 25% of teens participated in destruction of private or public property
- 30% of teens carried weapons, and 70% have seen weapons in school
- 22% of teens have been physically attacked.

regularly. Now, my children's elementary and middle schools have lock-down drills—in case a lunatic enters their school. On more than one occasion since the tragedy at Columbine our local high school has been evacuated for a bomb threat.

Ok, so you live in a tough time. That doesn't mean you have to join a street gang or become a junkie, does it? In your heart, God has put a desire to make a difference in an ungodly culture. He has made each of us for a purpose, and that includes you. Remember, the darker the night, the brighter the stars shine! You live at an awesome time to make a mark for God's glory.

You are not alone. Something is happening among students today. You and your peers, whether your generation is called "Millennials," "bridgers," "echoboomers," or "Net-Gens," (how about just "students") display a passion and zeal unseen in decades. I am referring to folks born about 1980–81 and later. Richard Ross, who initiated the "True Love Waits" sexual purity campaign, observed in 1998 that youth sixteen and under as a group seemed to be more serious about spiritual matters. Something is up—could it be the Lord is at work?

God Can Use One Person—Will You Be the One?

To celebrate our fifteenth wedding anniversary I took my wife Michelle to Hawaii. What a gorgeous place! The tropical beauty, the warm climate, the beaches, the palm trees, all this and more kept us enraptured. Michelle loved the shops, the nice restaurants, the pineapple plantations, the beautiful flowers, and oh so many rainbows. While there, I only wanted to do two things–snorkel, which is a trip in itself, and watch those bodacious surfer dudes hit the pipeline. The pipeline refers to an area on the north shore of Oahu where waves from the Pacific Ocean rise as high as a house to crash against the shore. For years I had watched those massive waves on television, but the spectacle seen live is hard to describe. To use surferspeak, those waves are gnarly, dude!

In fact, although lifeguards were everywhere, one thing quickly became obvious. Not everyone was allowed to surf the pipeline. No, this particular wave system off the Pacific Ocean which slammed the shore could only be engaged by professional, select surfers, because of the real danger the waves posed. This was not body surfing at Panama City, Florida, by any means! Only those who were courageous and equipped could enter the water.

The ocean of our culture is churning with dangerous waves. People are drowning in a sea of evil. The only people fit to surf these waves are those who have Jesus, the One Who can calm any storm, in their lives. We must crash into the waves of the world in order to proclaim the good news. If you are a Christian, God has saved you for a purpose–to make an impact in your generation. The Reformers in centuries past spoke of the "vocation" of every believer–the reality that every Christian (regardless of age) has been created for a special role in the kingdom of God that can be accomplished better by that individual (this means *you*) than any other person. In other words, God loves you so much, He has a place for you to serve Him that no one else can accomplish. That being said, some, not all, are called to unusual sacrifice, even death, for the cause of Christ. Most of us will live far calmer lives. But we are all called to radical obedience. If you know Jesus, He has placed in your heart a passion for Him. And, history is filled with the story of brave martyrs who died simply because they followed Jesus Christ.

Will you follow Him regardless the cost?

The First Great Awakening

Other generations have seen the impact of young people like you. For example, when America existed as thirteen colonies during the early 1700s, spiritual life grew very dull. Churches typically were boring, boring, *boring!* Key biblical truths, such as the uniqueness of Jesus and the need for personal salvation, often softened from neglect. Have you ever been to a church like that? Yet, God used people in special

> Some churches start their services at 11 o'clock sharp and end at 12 o'clock dull.
>
> —Vance Havner

ways to bring great revival to that generation in the early 1700s: people like John Wesley, George Whitefield, Jonathan Edwards, Count Zinzendorf, Howell Harris, and Gilbert Tennent. These and others like them became major leaders in one of the greatest revivals in history called the First Great Awakening. And, for many of them their greatest impact in the revival came while in their twenties or early thirties! In almost every case God began to work in their lives while teenagers. This movement of God affected young people more than anyone else. The impact of the work of God was so great on that generation that even such notable scholars as Perry Miller, history professor for many years at Harvard University, said the decade from 1740–50 was the most important in the history of our nation, and that was because of the First Great Awakening. Did I mention that Perry Miller was not a believer, by the way? Even a scholar who claimed no belief in Jesus recognized that one generation can have an impact on a nation for many generations following.

I have no doubt that the most overlooked aspect of revival is the role of youth. Few historians emphasize this, but when you read the accounts of people who lived in the middle of great revivals, they regularly emphasized how youth played a vital role. No less than Jonathan Edwards, a key leader in the First Great awakening best known for his sermon "Sinners in the Hands of an Angry God," stressed that awakenings particularly affected the younger generation. Concerning the effect of the First Great Awakening on youth in Northampton, Massachusetts, he commented (pardon the eighteenth century English!):

> God made it, I suppose, the greatest occasion of awakening to others, of anything that ever came to pass in the town . . . news of it seemed to be almost like a flash of lightning, upon the hearts of young people, all over town, and upon many others.[3]

Now, imagine if half your town got radically saved in less than a year as they did in Northampton! What if half your high school became radical and fanatical Christians this school year? You could see a change in your school couldn't you? By radical and fanatical I don't mean you have to act like an idiot, but simply to live with a passion for God above anything else. The revival in Northampton spread quickly to neighboring towns and greatly affected everyone. In fact, Edwards remarked further on the role of youth in this revival, while indicting older believers for their indifference:

> The work has been chiefly amongst the young; and comparatively but few others have been made partakers of it. And indeed it has commonly been so, when God has begun any great work for the revival of his church; he has taken the young people, and has cast off the old and stiff-necked generation.[4]

Stern words for our day as well! Now lest I be too hard on older folks, let me add that every great revival was also helped by the maturity of older believers. We need the wisdom of the aged *and* the zeal of youth.

Edwards actually served a church that had seen a series of revivals sweep across the community, largely influenced by young people, over decades. The movement in 1734–35 began when Edwards encouraged (okay, maybe scolded is more accurate) the youth to become more serious about the things of God. In particular he chided them for their frivolous attitude toward honoring the Lord's day. Imagine a pastor telling teenagers to get right with God, and they did! The youth were also affected greatly by the sudden death of a young man and then of a young married woman in their town. Edwards proposed that the young people begin meeting in small groups around Northampton. They did so with such success that many adults followed their example. The revival surfaced following a series of messages by Edwards on salvation.

The revival was so powerful that people on each street corner talked only about the Lord. Imagine going to school and hearing people only talking about Jesus. Half the town got saved in one year! What an awesome change it would take for that to occur. Fortunately, we serve an awesome God!

God's Vision for You

In Jeremiah 1, God told Jeremiah that He knew the prophet before he was even conceived. And, before his birth God had called him to be a prophet. God knew you before you were born as well, and God already had plans for you. Have you begun to understand God's vision for your life? Do you believe God could use you to play a role in His great work? Jeremiah doubted a bit, but God's call was certain. He has just as certainly called you, and will use you to His glory. Finding and living out God's purpose for you is the greatest adventure on the earth. It is not so much a roadmap as it is a relationship, so to find His vision, start by getting to know Him better. And, you can only get to know Him better once you have established a relationship with Him through what the Bible calls salvation.

Let me ask you a question: do you know Jesus Christ in a real, life-changing kind of a way? Or are you basing your relationship with God on such things as church involvement, or moral living, or something else? Christianity involves going to church, but that is not what makes you a Christian. It includes living morally, but genuine believers are more than that. Being a Christian means you have been *changed* by the power of the gospel. The Bible says, "If anyone is in Christ, he is a new creation" (II Corinthians 5:17). As a young man, just entering middle school, I realized what the Bible says is true: I was a sinner. We all are, you know (Romans 3:23). In fact, as a youngster your parents never had to teach you to be disobedient! It is in your nature, as it is in mine. So, because sin separated us from

God, Jesus Christ came to earth to live a sinless life and to die in our place. That is great love!

A little girl six years old had a rare blood disease. The only cure was to get a blood transfusion from a close family member who had beaten the disease. Her eleven year old brother was the perfect match. So, the family physician asked the young man if he would give his blood for his very sick sister. "Of course," the boy replied.

They laid the boy on a table, and took the blood. As soon as it was given to the sister she began to feel stronger. She was going to be fine! But, after a length of time the mother realized her son had not gotten up from the table. She asked the doctor to speak to the boy. When the doctor went into the room, he found the young man lying on his back, very tense, with his teeth clenched, and tears rolling down his temples. "What is wrong?" The doctor asked. "Doctor," the boy replied, "When am I going to die?" The doctor realized the brother thought giving his blood would cost his life. He pulled the boy up, hugged him, and said, "Oh, son, you are not going to die. You will be fine, and your sister is too!" Then the doctor asked the boy, "If you thought giving your blood would cost your life, why did you so freely give it for your sister?" The boy shrugged his shoulders and said, "Well, doctor, she is my little sister, and I love her!" Jesus loved you so much He died for you!

████████████ Vision made personal

Take a few minutes and read John 3 in your Bible. Can you say that you have come to know Jesus Christ in such a way that you can call it a *new birth*? Has Jesus Christ clearly changed your life? You are created in the image of God, and though sinful, Jesus loves you. He loves you so much He stretched out His arms and died for you. The Bible says, "If you confess with your mouth that Jesus is Lord, and believe in your heart God has raised Him from the dead, you will be saved" (Romans 10:9–10).

If you have never experienced the real, life-changing salvation that God offers you, now is the time to receive His gift of eternal life. You can do that through prayer, for God's Word says, "Whoever calls on the name of the Lord will be saved" (Romans 10:13). The Bible teaches that one comes to a personal relationship with God through Jesus by repentance (turning from your sin to live for God) and faith (putting your complete trust in Him).

If you are not certain of a real relationship with God, turn from your sins and from living for yourself, and give your life to God. You can offer the following prayer to God now:

> *Dear God,*
> *I need you in my life. I confess that I have sinned. I believe Jesus Christ died for me on the cross and rose again. I turn from my sin, please forgive me. Come into my life and take control. I will live for you. Amen.*

If you just said this to God, call your pastor, or youth pastor, or an adult you trust as a spiritual leader and tell them. You are now ready to live the life God made you to live!

If you are certain you are already saved, take a moment and thank God for saving you. He didn't have to, you know. But not only did He save you, but He planted deep inside you a vision to live radically for Him.

Chapter Two

Passion

For we cannot but speak the things
which we have seen and heard.
Acts 4:20

Let God set you on fire,
and people will watch you burn.
—John Wesley

MOST OF THE READERS OF THIS BOOK WILL LIKELY NOT FACE DEATH for your faith. There is a more pressing question for us: not, will we die for Jesus, but will we *live* for Him?

In these pages you will be reading about God's work among youth–from a young evangelist named Whitefield in the 1700s, to the teenage martyrs Rachel Scott and Cassie Bernall at the brink of the 21st century. Oh, that God would raise up a generation of students who live on fire for Him. On second thought, maybe He *is*.

A youth group from Southwayside Baptist Church, Fort Worth, was sitting near the back of the auditorium at the Wedgwood Baptist Church when the shooting began on that fateful night in September, 1999.

Adam Hammond, a Southwestern Seminary student and Southwayside's youth minister, yelled, "Get down, this is real!" as teens hit the floor to take shelter under the pews. Larry Gene Ashbrook had entered the church firing a handgun, screaming curses at Christians.

"I didn't know if my youth were OK and I felt totally helpless," Hammond said. "I just kept praying." Within minutes, he said, a young girl just behind Hammond's youth group was shot in the back. Soon a trail of blood covered the floor and then his clothes.

"When the first round was done I heard the clip hit the floor and he reloaded," Hammond recalled.

Then Ashbrook shouted, "Your religion [expletive]."

Jeremiah Neitz, a youth in Hammond's group, could not keep silent. "No, sir, it doesn't." He said as he turned to face the gunman.

"Yes it does!" cried a more irritated Ashbrook.

"No, sir, it doesn't."

Neitz stood facing Larry Gene Ashbrook hardly a pew-length away. "What you need is Jesus Christ," Neitz said. Ashbrook fired more shots, but not at Neitz. The youth's words seemed to confuse the gunman. He slumped into a pew at the rear of the sanctuary, with what witnesses described as a look of disbelief on his face. As he sat, Jeremiah stood.

Hammond tugged at Jeremiah's leg, trying to get him to take cover. Trey Herweck, a 24 year old seminary student, said Jeremiah looked fearless as he faced Ashbrook.

Ashbrook aimed the gun at Jeremiah's head. "Sir," Neitz said, "you can shoot me if you want. I know where I am going–I'm going to heaven." Hammond thought this would only enrage the gunman, making him shoot more people. A shot was fired–Hammond thought this signaled the death of Neitz. Instead, Ashbrook had put the gun to his own head, taking his life.

One person, and that person a youth only recently returning to God, stopped the killing. A young man passionate for Jesus stood courageously for his Master.[5]

Willing to Die, Ready to Live

The life and death of Jim Elliott stands as a sobering example of the agony and the ecstacy of service to God. Elliott epitomizes a young man sold out to God, a life abandoned to Him. Elliott, like Abel (Genesis 4), is a man who though dead still speaks. Elliot died to himself as a young man, and affected a generation of those now living. That is why his life can be called a life exhibiting a personal revival. He loved sports, but he worshiped Jesus, not a sports team. He had an interest in the opposite sex, and ultimately married a godly young lady named Elisabeth. He pursued his degree with all diligence, and even seemed to love studying Greek! But all these paled in comparison to his love for Jesus. You see, you can have many interests, but only one passion. You can have numerous commitments, but you can only surrender to One. You can enjoy several subjects, but that one thing you abandon yourself to is your God.

Elliott graduated from Wheaton College in 1949. During his senior year, he wrote: *He is no fool to give that which he cannot keep to gain that he cannot lose.* Those words would be prophetic, for seven years later, only in his twenties, he would give his earthly life for his eternal reward.

By his sophomore year at Wheaton, still a teenager, Jim became convinced that God was directing his life toward South America. In the summer following his junior year he wrote: "Glad to get the opportunity to preach the Gospel of the matchless grace of our God to stoical, pagan Indians. I only hope that He will let me preach to those who have never heard that name Jesus. What else is better in this life? I have heard of nothing better. 'Lord, send me!'"[6]

Don't misunderstand—Jim Elliott was not some bizarre character who fit in so poorly with his peers that he felt the need to escape to a foreign land. No, he was a champion wrestler, honor student, amateur poet, and was warmly admired by students at Wheaton. He was the BMOC, Big Man on Campus. If you think people who become preachers or missionaries are the nerds or outcasts, think again.

By the end of 1950 Jim began to sense the leadership of God to the Auca Indians in Ecuador. This primitive, hardly known tribe had been unreached despite other missionary efforts. They were so ruthless, even other Indian tribes steered clear of this hostile tribe. Missionaries, rubber trade workers, and Shell oil employees were some of the many killed by the Aucas. They were known by those who knew something of them as killers.

The words of Jim Elliot reflect his passion:[7]"We are still utterly ordinary, so commonplace, while we profess to know a power the 20th century does not reckon with. But we are harmless, and therefore unharmed. We are spiritual passivists, non-militants, conscientious objectors in this battle to the death with principalities program and powers in high places. Meekness must be had for contact with men, but brass, outspoken *boldness* is required to take part in the comradeship of the cross. The world cannot hate us, we're too much like its own. Oh that God would make us *dangerous*!"

Pete Fleming, one of the four men who would die with Jim Elliott in an effort to win the Aucas to Jesus, wrote:

> It is a grave and solemn problem; an unreachable people
> who murder and kill with extreme hatred. It comes to
> me strongly that God is leading me to do something

about it, and a strong idea and impression comes into my mind that I ought to devote the majority of my time to collecting linguistic data on the tribe and making some intensive air surveys to look for Auca houses....I know that this may be the most important decision of my life, but I have a quiet peace about it.[8]

One of the ways God helped Jim Elliott to develop such powerful faith was through the discipline of keeping a journal. Do you keep a daily spiritual journal? Countless believers have found this to be a great aid in their walk with Christ. Elliot's journals show an amazing depth of focus on the study of Scripture.

Read some of Elliot's journal entries:[9]

July 7, 1948,
> Psalm 104. Psalm 104:4: "He makes His ministers a flame of fire." Am I ignitable? God deliver me from the dread asbestos of "other things." Saturate me with the oil of the Spirit that I may be a *flame.* But flame is transient, often short-lived. Canst thou bear this, my soul, a short life?

This entry, written years before his death at the hands of the Aucas, demonstrated that Elliot was actually dead long before the spears pierced him. He had died to self long before.

January 31, 1949,
> [Senior year in college] Jeremiah 25, 26. Evening. One does not surrender a life in an instant–that which is life-long can only be surrendered in a lifetime.

November 18, 1949
> Just finished *Under a Thatched Roof* by Rosemary Cunningham, the story of a five-year term on the Xingo River of Brazil. Stirred for pioneer work again, like the

feeling I had on finishing [James] McNair's *Livingstone the Liberator* a couple years ago. O God, raise up a vanguard of young men to reach the untouched, the untouchables!

This entry reveals Elliot's growing conviction that God had called him to reach those who had never been reached for the Gospel.

In the summer of 1950 Elliot took a course in descriptive linguistics at the University of Oklahoma. This course would help him to work with South American tribes with no written language. By this time, he was convinced God had called him to go to Ecuador.

January 4, 1950
> I must not think it strange if God takes in youth those I should have kept on earth til they were older. God is peopling eternity, and I must not restrict Him to old men and women.

This journal entry shows Elliot's eternal perspective.

January 16, 1950
> Deserted all morning. Much time on my knees but no fervency or any desire for prayer.

This entry shows that Elliot, though possessing an unusual passion for God, had struggles in his devotion to the Lord as we all do.

Jim Elliott and four young companions, all in their twenties, journeyed to Ecuador to meet the Auca Indians. There they died. The Aucas attacked them, killing them with spears. The young missionaries had guns with them, but refused to shoot. They did not reach the Indians, but amazingly, their widows later came to Ecuador and reached the entire tribe for the gospel!

Years later, a young man traveling in Ecuador flew in a small plane over the country. The pilot knew of Jim Elliot's ministry. "When we fly over the place where Jim Elliot and the others died, show me," the man said to the pilot.

"I can't take you there," replied the pilot.

"Why not?"

"Because Jim Elliot did not die in Ecuador."

Perplexed, the young man remarked, "Yes, I know Jim Elliot died here in Ecuador."

"Jim Elliot's body expired in this country," the pilot said, "But Jim Elliot *died* while a college student at Wheaton College several years before. He yielded his life to God then, no matter the consequences."

You see, for Jim Elliot, the step from this life to the life beyond was a little one, because he walked so close to Jesus.

A Young Lady, a Spiritual Pastor, and a Young Coal Miner

Jim Elliott died to himself in college, and to this day has influenced thousands of young people to surrender all to the Lord. But you do not have to die for Jesus to make an impact, nor do you have to wait until college for God to use you.

Joseph Jenkins must have had lots of headaches—big, mean, migraines. After all, he was a spiritual man who served as pastor of a dead church in Wales, a part of the British Isles. In frustration he began a Young People's Meeting in November 1903 to battle the growing worldliness in his church. He figured if the older folks were dead, maybe

---

As a teenager, Evan Roberts dreamed of seeing God move in the lives of people. What kind of dreams do you have? Would they be dreams that honor the Lord?

the youth still had hope. At first the response was less than promising. Then, Jenkins was visited by a shy young girl following an evening service in January, 1904. The young lady, Florrie Evans, gave her life to Christ.

The following week, the first Sunday in February, Jenkins asked for testimonies during the Young People's Meeting following the morning service. Then, he asked for responses to the question, "What does Jesus mean to you?" That same young, poor Welsh girl spoke in a trembling voice: "If no one else will, then I must say that I do love the Lord Jesus Christ with all my heart." Unexpectedly, spontaneously, her sincere, earnest confession had the effect of a lightning strike of the Spirit in the congregation. Person after person arose and made full surrender to Christ. This simple, earnest testimony began in a big way what we call the great Welsh Revival of 1904–05.

News of the service spread throughout the area as young people testified in other churches. Within six months a growing sense of revival spread throughout surrounding areas. God changed the church, and changed the community, through the testimony of students! In September 1904 Seth Joshua, a respected evangelist, came to lead special services at Jenkins' church. Joshua related how "he had never seen the power of the Holy Spirit so powerfully manifested among the people as this place." Commenting further, he said on September 20: "I cannot leave the building until 12 and even 1 o'clock in the morning—I closed the service several times and yet it would break out again quite beyond the control of human power."[10] Awesome!

Taking the fire of God begun by a teenager's earnest testimony, Joshua traveled to another town, where a coal miner named Evan Roberts heard him at the last service. Evan Roberts' name is linked to the Welsh Revival of 1904–05, when 100,000 people came to Christ in that tiny nation in less than a year! His passion for revival began as a teenager. He provided a human spark to the work of God while in his twenties. Roberts came from a humble, religious family. The devout lad took a Bible everywhere as a child. Early in his life he dreamed of revival. While a young coal miner, a page of the Bible was scorched, the page at II Chronicles 6 where Solomon prayed for revival. Perhaps Evan saw this as prophetic, for when he became world-known, the Bible was displayed in photographs around the world.

Roberts followed Seth Joshua to hear him preach in yet another town, he had such a hunger for the things of God. The Thursday morning service closed with Joshua praying, "Lord. . . Bend us." Roberts went to the front, knelt, and with great anguish cried, "Lord, bend *me*." Reflecting on that prayer, Roberts later said the impact of his commitment had this effect: "I felt ablaze with a desire to go through the length and breadth of Wales to tell of my Savior; and had that been possible, I was willing to pay God for doing so."[11] God can use anyone with that kind of passion.

Immediately Roberts began to go to various towns to speak of his changed life. The presence of the Spirit was obvious, but demonstrated only a glimpse of a deeper work to come.

"Oh, Syd," Roberts said to his best friend Sydney Evans in late 1904, "We are going to see the mightiest revival that Wales has ever known—the Holy Spirit is coming just now." In great anticipation, he added, "We must get ready. We must get a little band and go all over the country preaching." Suddenly Roberts stopped, looked at Sydney, and said, "Do you believe that God can give us 100,000 souls now?"[12] Within six months, 100,000 were converted in Wales.

Roberts felt impressed to speak to his home congregation. On October 31 he took a train to his hometown of Loughor. He was allowed to speak only following the regular Monday night prayer service. Seventeen people remained to hear Roberts, all of them young people. The next day he spoke at a nearby town. On November 2 in nearby Moriah, Roberts began to speak about four key points for revival:

1. **You must put away any unconfessed sin.**
2. **You must put away any doubtful habit.**
3. **You must obey the Holy Spirit promptly.**
4. **You must confess Christ publicly.**

These became known as the "Four Points." Within one week much of Loughor had been changed. Young people gave testimonies about the greatness of God, and meetings lasted until four in the morning. God had come in power to Wales!

Real Passion made personal

Stop reading for a minute. Look up I John 1:9 in your Bible. In your heart, ask God if there are any unconfessed sins in your life. Maybe you need to write every sin on a sheet of paper. Go over Evan Roberts' Four Points as you pray. Ask God to reveal any relationships that do not honor Him. Then, write down any habit in your life that you question whether it is good or bad. When in doubt, leave it out! Take a few minutes to go back over each item you wrote down, and ask God to forgive you. Read I John 1:9, and claim the promise of God's forgiveness. Yield your life to God. When finished, confess your desire to obey the Holy Spirit. Commit yourself to tell others about Jesus. And thank God that He desires to use you!

Chapter Three
Impact

Go therefore and make disciples of all the nations, baptizing them in the name of the Father and of the Son and of the Holy Spirit, teaching them to observe all things that I have commanded you.

Matt. 28:19– 20a

That land is my home which most needs the gospel.

—Nicholas Zinzendorf, as a young man

IN MARCH OF 1998 I TOOK MY SON JOSH ON A TRIP TO ATLANTA during his spring break. We had a blast–hot dogs at the Varsity, a komodo dragon at the Zoo, a little shopping at Underground Atlanta, you get the idea. As we sat on the plane to head back to Raleigh, I read the headline on that day:

"Five Killed at Ark. School: 4 Students, Teacher Die In Ambush; 2 Classmates Held"

Westside Middle School in Jonesboro appeared to be a typical public school in a smallish city in Northeastern Arkansas. What happened on Tuesday, March 24, 1998, was anything but typical. The premeditated ambush on classmates by two boys, eleven and thirteen years old, sent shockwaves across the nation. These young cousins pulled the school fire alarm at Westside, hid behind trees with rifles and in camouflage gear, and began shooting as people filed out of the building. Boys barely older than my son killed five and wounded fourteen others. Why? Because one of the boys was upset with his former girlfriend.

Only three weeks earlier I had spoken at a church with a fabulous youth group. The students there seemed to have an unusual love for God. On the last night, I challenged the church to take copies of a gospel tract and share with someone the next week. The response was terrific, especially among the students. Some of the youth got my email address. They shared, as did their pastor, exciting stories of the days following. The bottom line is, in less than a week, four schoolmates, and one young person in the youth group, accepted Christ. In Jonesboro, Arkansas, four teens and a teacher died as a result of a horrible tragedy. Just three weeks earlier, five teens in South Carolina met Christ. You see, the gospel matters. Young people who share Jesus can make a great impact for Him.*

The situation in Jonesboro unfortunately was not a one time event. But *neither* was what happened with the youth group in South Carolina. Hopeful signs are around. God is up to something. Across the nation, and literally around the world, sparks are igniting which give hope on an otherwise bleak horizon. Maybe you can't stop all the violence

---

*   The above is taken from Alvin L. Reid, "If Youth Be Served," *SBC Life*, June 1998

in the schools, but you *can* change your world, one heart at a time. In a small church youth group, at a Christian club, in informal hangouts, increasing numbers of students are fed up with the cultural rot in our nation. Is God stirring your generation for a mighty revival?

God Is at Work

All around us we see signs, indicators, that the Spirit of God is at work. And, God evaluates young people differently than many adults do in the church today. Too often more mature Christians in churches treat young people as overgrown children who just might hold hope for the church in the future. However, our great God sees students as essential for what He is doing in the church today! The best way to see this is by looking at the incredible way God has used young people, many while still in their teens, to make an incredible impact on their times. Hopefully, as we find ourself in a new millennium, this book will help you to experience the mighty work of our God. Someone named Santyana once said those that don't learn from history are doomed to relive it. Ok, I think Santyana was a pessimist. I like to think that we can learn good lessons from the past as well.

The Bible and history are filled with examples of young people mightily used of God. Some were only in their teens, some in their early twenties. Josiah was a godly king who began his reign as a boy of eight! David gave Goliath a terminal headache while only a teen. Joseph began his difficult pilgrimage to greatness while a youth. Samuel moved into an intimate relationship with God which would guide him his entire life while only a lad. Timothy, who followed Paul as a major leader in the early church, was likely a youth when he began to assume leadership.

> A holy man is an awesome weapon in the hands of God.
> —Robert Murray McCheyne

George Whitefield–A Man Ablaze for God

If there is a unifying force among the student population in our country it is found in one word: PIZZA. Recently our family ate at a little pizza place near our home. The home-made flavor was especially good. Then, Josh got a piece of the dessert pizza. It was a collection of assorted chocolates, particularly laced with pounds of chocolate chips. Nasty! But of course he loved it. He was so impressed he told one of the waiters, "This pizza rules!"

Lots of things "rule" in this day: a certain singing group rules, soccer rules, the beach rules, on and on. Then you add the sports crowd, with their t shirts saying "Basketball is Life," or "Baseball is Life." If you are serious about fol-lowing Jesus, you know that while these things aren't bad, they don't rule, and they aren't life.

"God, give me a deep humility, a well-guided zeal, a burning love and a single eye, and then let men or devils do their worst!" This quote epitomizes the life of George Whitefield, who preached to thousands of people while in his early twenties. God in His greatness uses all kinds of people to bring glory to Himself. One thing is certain—the people He uses most are people who understand that *God* rules, and that *Jesus* is life. And, it is much more than a slogan to slap on a shirt. Look at people in the past who touched their generation, and you find people, regardless of their age or ability, who were passionate about God.

Some used by God are very gifted, some are completely unimpressive. Most of us have wondered at times some-thing like this: "If God radically saved Michael Jordan, what a great impact he would have for God." More times than not, however, God uses ordinary, normal people to do mighty things. God doesn't use somebodies, a friend of mine once says, He uses nobodies sold out to Him!

But sometimes, God takes a very gifted person and shapes him or her to fulfill a significant task. Such is the case with George Whitefield. You may have never heard of Whitefield, but at the young age of 24, he came to the

> Whitefield was a gifted speaker, with a great voice and a dramatic approach. The famous English actor of his day, David Garrick, said Whitefield could move people to tears by the way he said "Mesopotamia." Try doing THAT in your youth group!

American colonies to preach, and was soon the most popular man in the colonies! He preached to thousands of people wherever he went. By the time he was barely twenty he was preaching to huge crowds in his native land of England.

Whitefield lived from 1714–1770. He and John Wesley (1703–1791) and others were key leaders in a mighty revival called the Evangelical Awakening in England during the Eighteenth Century. Tens of thousands were radically saved, and the whole nation was affected. Wouldn't you love to be a part of something like that?

Whitefield met Jesus in a powerful conversion while a teen Like most teenagers, he pursued his own interests for most of his young life. Then, over time, he began to be more and more concerned about his relationship with God. He read a book called *The Life of God in the Soul of Man*. The book showed him he could not be converted by just trying to live a decent life. He wrote about its effect:

> God showed me that I must be born again, or be damned!
> I learned that a man may go to church, say prayers, ...
> and yet not be a Christian. . . .
>
> . . . God soon showed me, for in reading a few lines
> further, that 'true Christianity is a union of the soul with
> God, and Christ formed within us,' and from that mo-
> ment, and not till then, did I know I must become a new
> creature.[13]

Finally, George surrendered his life to God. He had no idea the kind of impact he would have for God.

Whitefield met John and Charles Wesley, and others while attending college at Oxford. They formed what we might call a Christian club today while there. Other students made fun of these early Jesus Freaks, calling them "Bible bigots" for their devotion to reading Scripture. The name that stuck to their group was the "Holy Club." The Holy Club was a Christian club that focused on reading of Scripture, fasting, prayer, and ministry. Ever been ridiculed for your love for Jesus? If you are serious about Jesus, some of your peers will think you are strange.

Although saved at eleven, I grew serious about my absolute devotion to Jesus as a sophomore in high school. On the sidelines of a spring jamboree football game, gazing through my face mask, I yielded myself to Christ, consecrating to do anything He asked. Immediately my faith was tested. Remember, if you seek to honor Christ, God will test you to bring out your best, but Satan will tempt you to bring out your worst! About two weeks later all the sophomore athletes had the wonderful privilege of going through a week of hazing known as initiation into the "P" club (P for the name of our school). I won't go into all the details, like eating a raw egg every morning (does the word "salmonella" mean anything to you?); I will just say it was not the most pleasurable experience of my life.

On Thursday night the experience reached its peak. That night, a big, hulking upperclassman who played tackle on the football team took a friend of mine, a strong Christian named Joel, aside. He told me to refer to Joel's mother with a profane term. Without even thinking, I replied, No!" He could not believe I would refuse. I thought he was about to rip my arms off and beat me with them. I told him I wanted to honor Jesus with my life, and I couldn't say such words. Joel also refused. We both received ridicule and were really scared. But guess what–in part out of that experience, Joel and I began a Fellowship of Christian Athletes at our school, and later began a Christian club which soon became the largest club on campus. The mocking of some so-called "friends" actually helped us to do something for God!

One of the most significant things you can do while in school is to participate in a Christian club, especially if that club focuses on winning unsaved students to Jesus. The Holy Club at Oxford developed relationships between the men who would become leaders in the Great Awakening in England and the American colonies. You never form a Christian club to bring in a great revival, but neither should you underestimate the impact such a small group can have on a campus, or even a nation. Certainly, the greatest long term impact of such a group is what is does to the members, helping them grow closer to Jesus.

Whitefield made seven trips on rickety little sailboats to the American colonies. Up and down the Atlantic coast he traveled, fanning the flame of revival wherever he went. He was only twenty-six years old in 1741 when the Great Awakening was at its peak! He spoke with a fire from heaven, thundering the gospel to the people. He once told a crowd: "You blame me for weeping, but how can I help it when you will not weep for yourselves, though your immortal souls are on the verge of destruction!... I did not come to tickle your ears; no, but I came to touch your hearts."[14]

We can learn from George Whitefield what it takes to be on fire for God. Have you ever been so excited for Jesus, I mean so excited you were ready to take on hell with a squirt gun, and then for some reason lost your passion for Jesus? We all have a tendency to do that at times. Here are some ways George kept his fire for God burning bright:

For one, *George hung around with those who had a similar hunger for God*. The Wesley brothers, John and Charles, influenced him greatly. A fellow who wasn't even a minister named Howell Harris encouraged George to get out of the church building and share Christ with people out in the fields. Because of that George reached thousands the churches had overlooked. When in America, he spent time with people who saw the hand of God touch in revival— Theodore Frelinghuysen, Gilbert Tennent, and Jonathan Edwards, to name only a few. If you run around with dogs, you are bound to get some fleas! We should spend much of our time with brothers and sisters who seek the hand of God.

George Whitefield lived a life of humility. He never sought to make a name for himself. He was unusually gifted, but simply sought to burn brightly for Jesus. Once he was crossing the Atlantic Ocean, and following a storm his boat took on too much water. Many feared the boat would sink. About that time another ship came alongside Whitefield's. When the captain of the boat of the healthy vessel discovered the great preacher Whitefield was on board the waterlogged ship, he offered Whitefield a ride on his. However, George refused, because he believed he was no better than anyone else on his boat. All he wanted to do was to make an impact for Jesus.

He demonstrated courage and determination. On another voyage, three small ships traveled together. Instead of laying back and resting on the trip, George preached–to all three boats at once! He never ceased to speak the name of Jesus despite opposition. Once, he preached near London. Some who hated the Gospel beat a drum in an attempt to drown him out. Concerning the abuse he took that day, he wrote later in his journal: "I was blessed of God today to have rocks, and stones, and pieces of dead cats thrown at me."[15] Now that is gross! Some folks got so mad at his preaching, they cut up a poor cat and threw its remains at Whitefield as he preached (sorry to all you cat lovers). Yet preach he did, and hundreds came to Christ that day!

More than anything else, *George Whitefield was a man on fire for God.* He loved to share the gospel, because this was his passion. He once said, "God forbid that I should travel with anyone a quarter of an hour without speaking to them about Christ."[16] He would not talk to a person *fifteen minutes* without sharing Jesus. This was a man who preached to thousands. He never let that go to his head. He never had this thought, "Since I am such a big-shot preacher, I don't have to talk to anyone during the day–I can do my own thing." No, he was so on fire for God that Jesus just oozed out everywhere he went. If Jesus lives in you, it ought

---

The D.C. Talk CD Jesus Freak has a line in it we should all heed.

"The greatest single cause of atheism is Christians who acknowledge Jesus with their lips, and deny Him with their lives. That is what an unbelieving world finds unbelievable . . ."

to be so apparent that if a mosquito bit you, it would fly around singing "there is power, power, power in the blood!" Okay, that is a bit silly, because mosquitoes can't tell such things. But people can. Let your passion for God grow.

◼ Impact made personal

Take a few minutes and read Proverbs 3:5–6. Solomon, who wrote these words, wrote many helpful thoughts in the Proverbs. Keeping a spiritual journal yourself may not create a wealth of wisdom like Solomon wrote, but it sure can help your own walk with God.

George Whitefield, along with many great Christians in history, kept a personal spiritual journal. One of the best spiritual disciplines you can have is to keep a spiritual journal. Write what is going on in your life–the blessings, the sorrows, the prayers, the opportunities, the disappointments. In particular, write your dreams. Over time, you can look back over your journal and be encouraged at how God has worked in your life. Make this a part of your daily devotional time. By the way, your relationship to Jesus will never grow past your devotional life. I can promise you this, your impact for God will be helped by the keeping and reading of a journal.

Chapter Four

Purpose

Here am I, send me.
—Isaiah the prophet

I believe the world is upon
the threshold of a great religious revival,
and I pray that I may be allowed
to help bring this about.
I beseech all those who confess Christ
to ask Him today, upon their knees,
if He has not some work for them to do now.
He will lead them all as He has led us.
He will make them pillars of smoke by day
and pillars of fire by night
to guide all men to Him.
—Evan Roberts[17]

YEARS AGO A PSYCHOLOGIST NAMED ABRAHAM MASLOW DISCOVERED
what he called a hierarchy of needs. What he meant was
that, no matter what background, nationality, or financial
status, everyone had certain needs such as food, shelter,
and a sense of safety. I think Maslow was right, but he did
not go far enough, because everyone also has another need—
to know God and to make a difference with the life God

gives. Another person, mathematician Blaise Pascal, was more on the mark when he observed that every person has a God-sized vacuum, a God-shaped hole as a recent Audio Adrenaline song put it. Only Jesus can fill that hole. However, He does more than fill it. He gives each person who receives Christ a passion to live out God's purpose.

I was reminded of this recently at a DiscipleNow I led. About 225 teenagers met for a weekend at the Wildwood Baptist Church near Atlanta, Georgia. Wildwood had established an outstanding youth ministry in a growing, evangelistic church. This weekend was different from others the church had held, however. Instead of taking the youth miles away to a big extravaganza, and playing all manner of games, the weekend featured large group times with expository preaching, a day filled with intentional personal evangelism, and much time spent in prayer and self-examination. You are probably thinking laser tag sounds like more fun than this, but the students *loved* it! In fact, the one extra event, a contemporary Christian concert, was postponed on Friday night because God so stirred the youth in the large group time. The large group time featured no games either, just some excellent praise and worship singing followed by a message. And not a little sermonette for Christianettes who smoke cigarettes; no, the messages each session went from 30–40 minutes. I know because I preached them! After each session the students went into small group time focusing on serious self examination. On Saturday, students did evangelism projects from giving away batteries for smoke detectors, to giving away bread, to visiting nursing homes, to cleaning toilets! While doing these the students shared Christ and gave away tracts. The students got so excited that many begged to keep witnessing even when the scheduled time was up. Over twenty-five students met Christ that weekend. And get this—nearly all the students made a public commitment, including signing their names, to pray daily and intensively for twenty-eight days following the weekend.

Following the weekend a public school principle called the student minister, not to complain, but to ask what had happened to the students. He saw a clear difference in the teens who had gone to the weekend, and he loved the change! God continued to work in the students for weeks following the weekend.

This illustrates what I am trying to say. When students, like yourself, begin to understand God's purpose for your life, which comes through devotion to His Word, through intentional prayer, and by telling others about Jesus, students learn that serving Christ moves from being boring to a blast! Students at Wildwood did not complain, they rejoiced in their opportunity to honor God.

There were three keys to the weekend. First, leaders prayed intensively for 28 days prior to the weekend, followed by a 28 day commitment afterwards. When we pray, God works. Second, the focus was not on games but on God, not on playing but on God's purposes. Preaching was given preeminence over activities. Please understand, games are not evil, and I love to play around, but they are inferior to the joy of pleasing Jesus. Third, evangelism was given a great priority.

God Uses Us in Spite of Our Imperfections

The youth at Wildwood, like you and your friends, had no special ability or gifts. Many had never witnessed before and were very nervous. God used them, and He will use you, despite your weaknesses. Have you ever noticed how the great saints in history, and even well known spiritual leaders today, are presented in such a way as to make them larger than life, as if they had some kind of holy glitter showered on them? Truth is, they are all regular folks, just folks God chose to use mightily. They made mistakes, struggled with sin, and served God in spite of their weaknesses. You are just as much a child of God as they were. You have the same Jesus, the same love of God, and a purpose from God.

A fire chief brought together his men to give them their assignments around the fire station. "Joe, you are to mow the lawn. Jim and Bill, you wash the fire trucks. Sam, you man the phone. Ricardo, cook the meals. Malcolm, you help with the dishes."

"Ok, chief," said Jim, "We all know what our jobs are."

"No!" said the chief. "You only have one job, and that is to put out fires. Your specific assignment is to wash the trucks, but all of us have one job—to save lives!"

You and I have one job—to follow Jesus. We each have different assignments—minister, teacher, student, on and on. But our job remains the same. And, the amazing thing is that God uses each of us despite our weaknesses.

Exhibit A is David Brainerd. Brainerd's life has led countless numbers of believers to follow his example as a missionary. Yet, according to Jonathan Edwards, his al-most-father-in-law (David died while engaged to Edwards' daughter), he struggled with depression his whole life. To put it simply, Brainerd was a worrywart. See, here is a young man greatly used of God, who worried. God uses people, warts and all! He will use an unusually talented person like Whitefield, or an insecure person like Brainerd. Regardless of what you think are blemishes, God can still use you. Spurgeon said it best, "God hits good licks with crooked sticks!"

Brainerd had a second vice according to Edwards—he tended to be a workaholic. Such a tendency contributed to his early death (he died just before turning 30). He took the old saying "I'd rather burn out than rust out" seriously. Unfortunately, he *did* burn out as a young man. Despite his weaknesses, he is an example of a young man totally sold out to Jesus. All of us are a work in progress. Why not offer all of yourself to God, including your faults?

In a familiar passage used regarding revival, II Chronicles 7:14 tells us one of the marks of revival is that God's people humble themselves. Few in history have demonstrated a more humble, self-effacing life than David Brainerd. He lived less than 30 years, but his life still touches others. He did more in his twenties than most do in seventy or eighty years to the glory of God. He gives a great example as to why you need to serve Jesus *now*, and not wait until you are older.

Brainerd was born on April 20, 1718, and died in 1747. He would have fit in well with your generation, marked by homes in which one or both biological parents are missing. His father died before his tenth birthday, and his mother passed away when he was only fourteen. If you come from a broken home or live in a single parent or step-family environment, let Brainerd's example encourage you—God will use you. God's grace will trump your past.

Spiritually, his interest in God ran hot and cold throughout his teen years. At the age of twenty he began to get serious, reading his Bible completely two times that year. Ok, he didn't have such distractions as MTV, Sega, or Nintendo, but still he was obviously searching. The carelessness he saw in many who came to be Christians bothered David. As time passed, he wrestled with God inside (by the way, if you wrestle with God, God always wins). He became so burdened about the sin in his life that he commented he feared the ground might open up at any moment and suck him into the pit of hell. Finally, on July 12,

1739, he was radically saved, experiencing the peace only God gives.

A minister named Ebenezer Pemberton influenced young Brainerd to give his life to evangelizing the Indians. "My great concern," Brainerd wrote, "was for the conversion of the Indians to God."[18] When very few cared at all about the Indians and their need for Christ, Brainerd considered it a *privilege* to be with the Indians. Brainerd's sacrificial commitment to reach the Indians was blessed by God. On one occasion, for example, the Susquehannah Indians demonstrated unusual brokenness from Brainerd's preaching—drunkards bowed in repentance, while young and old were broken under the force of the Spirit. Jonathan Edwards admired Brainerd. Edwards' daughter Jerusha was engaged to the young preacher. Unfortunately, Brainerd died just before his thirtieth birthday from tuberculosis. Brainerd's *Diary* has influenced countless believers to live a sacrificial life. It played a key role in the life of Henry Martyn, the great missionary to India.

Someone has well said that you measure the greatness of a person by what it takes to discourage him. Brainerd, in extremely difficult conditions, continued to serve faithfully the Lord, even through he struggled with depression.

I received this encouraging email following a time when I taught our youth at church how to share their faith. It is from a father who is rightfully proud of his young son:

> I just wanted brag on the Lord for a second. Brian (age 13) went to youth group at our church last night . . . he has been blessed with a really good one. The leaders really encourage him, and the others, to follow Christ with all their hearts. Last night, one of my seminary profs talked to them about sharing their faith with others. He gave them a handful of Gospel tracts to use as the Lord

led. (thanks Dr. R) Brian told me that he wanted to give them to 3 of his teachers at his middle school that he likes a lot but hasn't seen anything in their lives that would make him think that they know Jesus personally. He did that today, but only after he shared the information in the tracts with 2 other kids at the school first!! Praise our faithful God for working in the lives of kids even when their dads do not give them the example God wants them to. Although I am extremely proud of Brian for his courage and his compassion for those who do not know Christ, I have been made very aware that only God could do this in his young life. For those who have been praying for the kids, I wanted to give you this most encouraging update.

God bless all
Lee

Oh, that God would raise up a generation of thirteen year olds like that! Come to think of it, maybe He is. David Brainerd served God in humility, and saw God work mightily. That is why they called his day a great awakening.

Rachel's Story

Rachel Scott was one of the young martyrs at Columbine High School. Following her death, her father Darrell observed that the Columbine tragedy would be as memorable for this generation as the assassination of president John Kennedy was for his:

"April 20, 1999 for this generation is when time stood still." He added, "Tragedy is triumph in disguise . . . God is in control . . . He is not asleep when tragedy occurs . . . God was not caught off-guard with the tragedy of Columbine."[19]

Rachel Scott was a normal teenager with normal struggles, yet one who abandoned herself to God in her teen years. Her diary recorded her growth and struggles:

March 1, 1998: "Dear God, sometimes when I'm craving your spirit nothing happens. I stand there with my hands stretched towards heaven crying out your name and nothing happens."

Although Rachel struggled in her faith, just eight days later she was beaming, strong, and she wrote: "I want to feel You in my heart, my mind, my soul, my life. I want heads to turn in the halls when I walk by. I want them to stare at me watching and wanting the life that You have put in me. I want you to overflow my cup with Your Spirit. I want so much from You. I want You to use me reach the unreached. . . . I have such a desire and passion to serve, but I want to do that *now*. I want to know and serve You *now*. I want heads to turn *now*. I want faith like a child *now*. I want to feel you in my heart, mind, and soul *now*. I want you in my life *now*. I'm crying out to You Father asking for Your Spirit now. I thank You I have You for all the blessings in my life. Your child, Rachel Joy."

April 20, 1998, one year to the day before the Columbine tragedy, Rachel wrote: "Its like I have a heavy heart and this burden upon my back. I don't know what it is. There is something in me that makes me want to cry and I don't know what it is. Things have definitely changed. Last week was so hard. . . I lost all of my friends at school now that I have begun to walk my talk. They make fun of me. I don't even know what I have done. I don't have to say anything and they turn me away, but you know what, it is all worth it to me because I am not going to apologize for speaking the name of Jesus. I'm not going to hide the light God has put into me. If I have to sacrifice everything I will. I will take it. If my friends have to become my enemies for me to be with my best friend Jesus, then that is fine with me."

Rachel gave herself to God to do with her as He desired. On May 2, 1998, Rachel wrote, "This will be my last year Lord. I have gotten what I can. Thank You."

About this time Rachel talked with three of her friends, her sister and her cousin saying that she would not live to be old enough to get married. Rachel had drawn a picture of the Christian fish with the verse inside that states, "Greater love has no man then this, that a man lay down his life for a friend." On the reverse side is a picture of a rose that has a number of drops of liquid falling off of it. The rose is growing out of a Columbine plant. After she drew this picture Rachel wrote this poem at the bottom: "Things untold, things unseen, one day all these things will come to me. Life of meaning, life of hope, life of significance is mine to cope. I have a purpose, I have a dream. I have a future or so it seems."

Listen to the words of Rachel Scott's father, speaking before the United States Congress. Let the passionate plea of a brokenhearted father be the rallying cry for you to take action:

> What has happened to us as a nation? We have refused to honor God, and in doing so, we open the doors to hatred and violence. And when something as terrible as Columbine's tragedy occurs-politicians immediately look for a scapegoat .... We do not need more restrictive laws. Eric and Dylan would not have been stopped by metal detectors. No amount of gun laws can stop someone who spends months planning this type of massacre. *The real villain lies within our own hearts. ... The young people of our nation hold the key. There is a spiritual awakening taking place that will not be squelched!*

We do not need more religion. We do not need more gaudy television evangelists spewing out verbal religious garbage. We do not need more million dollar church buildings built while people with basic needs are being ignored. We do need a change of heart and a humble acknowledgment that this nation was founded on the principle of simple trust in God!

As my son Craig lay under that table in the school library and saw his two friends murdered before his very eyes—He did not hesitate to pray in school. I challenge every young person in America and around the world to realize that on April 20,1999 at Columbine High School-prayer was brought back to our schools. Do not let the many prayers offered by those students be in vain. . . .

My daughter's death will not be in vain. The young people of this country will not allow that to happen.

Is he right? Will you not let that happen? Don't focus on what you cannot do for God. Focus on what He can do through you. He made you for a special, wonderful purpose. Find God's purpose and live to the glory of God.

▐ Purpose made personal

Take your Bible and read Jeremiah 29:11–13. God created you with a specific purpose in mind, a purpose that no other person in the history of the world can accomplish. You are pretty special! You find God's purpose by finding Him. God's will is not so much a roadmap as it is a relationship. So enjoy the journey of getting to know God, and as you travel the road, look for His purpose in your life.

Do you have a sense of purpose right now? Do you have an idea of where God is leading? Write down where you believe God wants you in 10 years. If you are clueless, write what you would love to be doing in terms of your relationship with God in 10 years. What must you do now to get you there?

Chapter Five

Missions

For I am not ashamed
of the gospel of Christ,
for it is the power of God to salvation
for everyone who believes,
for the Jew first and also for the Greek.
—Paul in Romans 1:16

We can do it if we will.
—Missionary Samuel Mills,
proposing a mission to Asia
while a college student

MY BROTHER SENT ME A VIDEO ONCE CALLED *Stomp out Loud.* IT shows a traveling troupe of percussionists/dancers with the incredible ability to put on one of the most entertaining shows I have ever seen using such common items as push brooms, basketballs, or spare automobile parts. Working as a group, they make the most incredible music (yes, I said music). Okay, I have tried to think of a way to insert their sound in this book, but I give up. Suffice it to say that you won't believe the harmony and rhythm you can get

> Jim Elliott once called missionaries
> "a bunch of nobodies trying to exalt somebody."

from a bunch of trash cans or sewer pipes until You see it. They are definitely one group that is in sync!

Two millennia ago Jesus gathered together a band of followers as unlikely as the scene I just described. He had everyone from a tax collector to a zealot. He had no professional ministers, and even had a traitor in the crowd. Imagine a church being led by an IRS agent, a closet agnostic, and a member of a grunge band. Well, maybe the comparison is not perfect, but you get the idea.

Yet Jesus took that band of believers, that den of disciples, that covey of Christians, and starting with them, changed the world.

Missions Mania

God has used unlikely groups in similar ways since. At the turn of the nineteenth century, God took a group of ordinary college students, who were stuck under a big stack of hay during a rainstorm, and gave them a vision to reach the world. The result? The modern foreign missions focus in America. The leader of that group was a guy named Samuel Mills, who saw God move in a great revival called the Second Great Awakening.

Students in modern history have played a greater role in missions than any other group. And, one of the marks of powerful revival historically is the sharp rise in the number of young people surrendering to full time Christian service in general and to foreign missions in particular. God calls *every* believer to serve Him; He sets apart *some*

> If God changed your schedule, if He allowed some "storm" in your life, what might be the result? Joni Earickson Tada experienced a dramatic change of schedule. As a teenager, she was diving into the ocean when she hit a shallow place unexpectedly. From that day forward she has been a paraplegic. As a result, Joni has become one of the greatest inspirational leaders in Christianity in the twentieth century. You may not have such a dramatic change, but if your plans get altered, please let God use the change to open fresh doors of service to Him.

to serve Him vocationally. Could God be calling you in that manner?

Samuel Mills was a PK (that's a "preacher's kid") from Torrington, Connecticut. God touched the congregation there with revival in 1798. Young Samuel never got over those days. Have you seen God do something incredible in your church? Never forget it! His hunger to be used by God increased as he matured. After enrolling at Williams College in Massachusetts, a powerful awakening came to the campus in 1804–06.

One of the marks of revival is a burden to pray. Samuel and a small group of students began to meet twice weekly for prayer. Do you have any friends with whom you can meet to pray? Not a bad idea! On a warm August day in 1806, the sky grew dark, the thunder rolled, and the heavens opened in a tremendous rainstorm. The group was meeting for prayer outside, so the storm drove the group to seek shelter. They climbed in a large haystack, a huge mound of hay gathered into a massive pile. Sheltered from the wind and rain at the haystack's side, the men continued in prayer. As they met in the storm, Samuel Mills suggested to his peers that they plan to go to India to share Christ. In the years since, historians have referred to the meeting as the "Haystack Revival." As a result of that one day, when their schedule was rearranged by the weather, these young men began a process that led in 1808 to form an organization to study and pray for missions. After seminary graduation, Mills and others of the "Brethren" (their group's name) asked the General Association of Massachusetts to send them to India as missionaries. This Association formed the American Board of Commissioners for Foreign Missions on June 28, 1810. This was the first official foreign missions organization in the United States. The first missionaries included Adoniram Judson, Samuel Nott, Luther Rice, Gordon Hall, and Samuel Newell. Mills stayed behind in part because of his ability to promote the cause of world missions in America.

The American Board of Commissioners for Foreign Missions began in 1810. Two of the first missionaries, Adoniram Judson and Luther Rice, became Baptists while en route to Burma. Rice formed the General Missionary Convention of the Baptist Denomination in the United States for Foreign Missions in 1814.

Samuel journeyed 3,000 miles through across America promoting overseas mission work. His work was influential in beginning the American Bible Society. In 1817 Mills helped form the American Colonization Society. So, the modern day missions movement in the United States can be traced in large part to revival and students.

Hampden-Sydney

The campus of Hampden-Sydney College in Virginia was actually the first in a series of college revivals. The fertile field of young students played a pivotal role beginning about 1787. Maybe you attend a public school and face ridicule for your faith. Let's be honest, you may be attending a private, "Christian" school and be criticized for your love of Jesus. Well, four young men—William Hill, Carey Allen, James Blythe, and Clement Read—feared literal attacks from the pagan student body, so they met secretly in the forest to pray and study. When they were discovered, the other students ridiculed them so much it almost caused a riot! President John Blair Smith heard of the situation and was ashamed by the whole scene. He invited the four students and others to pray with him in his parlor. Before long God began to move. One eyewitness said, "half of the students were deeply impressed and under conviction, and the revival spread rapidly through the college and to surrounding counties."[20]

Yale College

The Yale College revival began under the leadership of president Timothy Dwight, the grandson of Jonathan Edwards. Dwight came to the school when it was filled with infidelity. He began to preach against unbelief in the college chapel, and by 1797 a group of students formed to improve moral conditions. After more time passed characterized by prayer, a powerful spiritual movement came through the school in the spring of 1802. A third of the student body was converted. Goodrich wrote of the change in attitude on campus:

> The salvation of the soul was the great subject of thought, of conversation, of absorbing interest; the convictions of many were pungent and overwhelming; and "the peace of believing" which succeeded, was not less strongly marked.[21]

Bennett Tyler collected twenty-five eyewitness accounts of pastors during the Second Great Awakening. No less than twenty revival reports described the role played by young people. Ten accounts noted that the revivals started with the youth, and five documented the revival in their area effected young people more than any other group. Only one account out of twenty-five asserted there were no youth involved.

Over in Scotland, Robert Murray McCheyne, witnessed powerful revival in Dundee, Scotland. Converted July 8, 1831, McCheyne died before he turned thirty, yet God used him mightily. He spent great time in prayer and six hours daily in visitation. McCheyne's life has influenced generations of men of God. In Dundee, Scotland, McCheyne prayed in 1839, "God, make me as holy as a saved sinner can be."[22]

One of the most exciting efforts in recent days among the group of believers known as Southern Baptists is the call to young people to give up a semester, a summer, or a year of their lives to devote to missions work. If you have ever been on a mission trip you know the excitement of seeing lives changed and people encouraged by your efforts. Would you pray about giving up some of your schedule to devote full-time to the Lord?

Marks of Revivals Concerning Students

Certain features of past revival movements can be seen in relation to students:

1. In almost every case in history, young people played a prominent role in revival.
2. In times of revival evangelism is a priority, often fueled by the zeal of youth.

3. Youth touched by God in seasons of revival provide some of the most effective leaders for the church in the years following. Even a brief time of revival on a college campus can change the lives of the students there in such a way as they are never the same again.

   Wheaton College experienced a season of revival in March, 1995. Sharon Beougher, wife of professor Tim Beougher, attended some of the services. The first night, a regular Sunday evening service which began at 7:30 PM continued until 6:00 AM the next morning! Hundreds and hundreds of students met again the next four nights until around 2:00 AM, confessing their sins and getting right with God. After the first night Sharon went to the local YMCA to swim with an older friend. As Sharon shared what God had done the night before, her friend began to weep. "Sharon," this godly lady said, "I was a student at Wheaton when revival came in 1950. I have never been the same since I saw God move in those days." When you see the fire of God fall, you are never the same!

4. Brokenness for sin and radical obedience, which mark all true revivals, are prominent among youth. At Wheaton, students lined up for hours to confess their faults to one another. The second night, students began to bring CDs, magazines, alcohol, cigarettes, and other things that dishonored God from their dorm rooms. Five large garbage bags were filled with the stuff they brought. They were serious about forsaking anything that might cause them to dishonor the Lord!

5. In revival movements, multitudes of young people enter the ministry, or surrender to full-time missions service. The final night of services at Wheaton that March or 1995, two to three hundred students surrendered to full time Christian service. Most gave their lives to go to the mission field.

Missions made personal

Turn in your Bible to Acts 1:1–8. There is a sense in which every believer has the call to be a missionary, as we all are called to be witnesses. Still, the great need in the world is to get the gospel to the millions and millions who are not reached. I am referring especially to those in other nations where the gospel is not or cannot be openly preached. There are a variety of ways you can be involved in international missions:

- Take a short term missions trip with your church (you will *never* be the same)

- Give up a semester, a summer, or a year to serve overseas as a short term missionary

- Support through your finances and your prayers missionaries already on the field

- Perhaps God is calling you to be a champion for Him by giving you the honor of serving as a career missionary. If God called you to the ministry, either here or abroad, you have been given a great honor from Him!

Chapter 6

Excitement

When they saw
the boldness of Peter and John,
and perceived that they were
uneducated and untrained men,
they marveled;
And they realized that
they had been with Jesus.
Acts 4:13

Why should the devil
have all the good music?
Larry Norman song

OUT OF THE ASHES OF EVIL AT COLUMBINE HIGH SCHOOL CAME
the discovery that the gunmen were fellow classmates of
their victims. They had become so tainted by evil that they
laughed and cracked jokes while they shot their peers. Do
you ever think that people filled with such rage are simply
beyond the reach of salvation? Well, think again. God has
the power to do the impossible, even to the point of reaching the most unlikely. Dean is a good example.

In the early 1970s Dean and his girlfriend traveled across the southern United States, high on drugs of filled with alcohol most of the time. At one point they were arrested in Mobile, Alabama, and spent time in jail.

While there Dean could not get any drugs, so he became desperate for anything, including cigarettes. He had no way of getting any, so he began scraping up the cigarette butts off the floor discarded by the other inmates. Stuck in jail, with nothing to do, he also began to read a Gideon's Bible. He discovered the thin pages of the Bible were perfect for making cigarettes! So, he began to take the bits of tobacco at the end of the cigarette butts and roll them so he could smoke. Now, remember, he was lost, so he was clueless about the Word of God.

Until he began to read it. By the grace of God, he started reading the Gospel of John. He did this while he was smoking pages from the book of Leviticus! So there he sat, smoking Leviticus and reading John, and he gave his life to Christ!

When he was released he discovered his girlfriend had also met the Lord while in jail. Today, Dean is serving the Lord in the ministry. Radical, huh? Well, in the early seventies God saved a lot of strange looking young people. In fact, many young adults who had dropped out of society in the 1960s met the Lord. The change was so radical that they were called Jesus Freaks!

At the same time, God was stirring less strange young people. Asbury College in Kentucky experienced a powerful revival in 1970. In churches across America, youth choirs swelled in numbers as youth musicals gave teenagers a way to spread the gospel in a medium they loved.

God was up to something! All this was part of what became known as the Jesus Movement. It was called the

Jesus Movement because it simply focused on Jesus—on His power to save, and on His return. The big saying then among teenagers was "One Way!" Often this was yelled while an index finger was pointed into the sky, indicating the uniqueness of Jesus as the only true Savior.

A Christian Youth Counterculture

The Jesus Movement saw thousands of teenagers radically changed in the late 1960s and early 1970s. Evangelist Brad Jurkovich speaks to many thousands of teenagers every year. Brad recently described a T-shirt a radically saved Christian brother wore. It had no words, no "WWJD," no "No Jesus-No Peace/Know Jesus-Know Peace," none of that. No, that shirt merely portrayed a scene in a frame. The picture depicted a great school of fish of all shapes and sizes, all going in one direction. In the middle of that school of fish, a singular fish faced the opposite direction. This fish was unlike all the others. It was the Christian symbol ⊂×. The fish demonstrated in a stark image how the Christian life goes against the flow.

The Jesus Movement refers to the swelling numbers of youth in the early seventies who went against the flow – against the flow of so many youth who reacted to society by dropping out or experimenting with drugs on the one hand, and against the staleness of so many churches who had lost their passion for God on the other. Thousands of people came to Christ from lifestyles of drug addiction. Also, even more youth got a fresh dose of excitement in their churches. I have lost count of the numbers of people in ministry today over 40 (you know, over the hill) who look back to what God was doing in the early seventies as being the most important time in their lives spiritually.[23]

Let's Get Excited!

"Give me a J!"

"Give me an E!"

"Give me an S!"

"Give me a U!"

"Give me an S!"

"What does that spell?"

"JESUS!"

Jesus cheers, mass ocean baptisms, coffeehouse ministries, Christian rock and roll music, and unashamed personal witnessing characterized the early 1970s in the lives
of many young people. In the midst of the controversy in
American society in the late 1960s and early 1970s over
civil rights, nuclear weapons, and the war in Vietnam, God
moved. The Jesus Movement is best known for the so-called
"Jesus Freaks"–hippies, runaways, druggies and others who
were radically changed by the love of Christ. Go back to
1970 and 1971 and you will find the Jesus Movement on
the cover of major news magazines from *Time* to *Newsweek*
to *Life*. By the way, do you know what a Jesus freak is? It is
someone who loves Jesus more than you! Seriously, some
can be too zealous for the Lord without wisdom; however,
most of us are not *too* on fire for God!

The Jesus Movement included more than the Jesus
Freaks. Young people in churches of all denominations were
affected. The most common way the movement affected
churches was in the massive youth choirs and youth musicals (*Good News, Celebrate Life, Tell It Like It Is*, etc.) that
exploded across the country. In the early seventies, most of
the time the youth choir *was* the youth group. I came to
Christ in 1970 in a church which saw many hippie-types

get radically saved. We even started a coffeehouse, calling it the "One Way Christian Night Club." Later, I was in a church as a teen which averaged just over 200 in attendance, but had a youth choir of 70 teens. Also, in our small church, we had youth retreats every winter and summer, and had to cut off the attendance sometimes at 100, and even had to turn away some kids.

I have had pastors ask me, how did your church get so many youth to attend the retreats? My answer – we didn't, *God* did.

> Imagine if you had a camp or retreat when the number of teens that went equaled half the number of your weekly attendance. How many students would that be?

The Jesus Movement presented a unique, youth-driven awakening. This reality affected it negatively in that it tended to be driven by emotion and was at times superficial. Still, while not a "great" awakening, it is hard to imagine the contemporary church at the start of the third millennium without it's effects. The entire contemporary church movement, and in particular praise and worship choruses (and Christian rap, rock, and others which tend to annoy numbers of formerly young people), owes much to the Jesus Movement.

God Works in Mysterious Ways

Sometimes God does things in a unique way just to remind us He is still God. Like having Joshua march around Jericho to gain a victory in battle. Like using a stuttering, sheepherding runaway like Moses to lead His people. Like taking a guy named Saul who persecuted Christians for a living and changing him into the Apostle Paul. The unlikely place where the Jesus Movement began at least somewhat was Haight Ashbury, the Mecca of the California drug culture. Ted Wise led a movement in Haight Ashbury that saw "flower children" turn from drugs to Jesus. In Southern California the movement began simultaneously under the ministry of Chuck Smith at Calvary Chapel, Costa Mesa, and Lonnie Frisbee. Frisbee opened the House of Miracles coffeehouse under Calvary Chapel's sponsorship.

The best known feature of the Jesus Movement was the upraised index finger accompanied by the cry of "One Way." The young people saved during this time were evangelistic to the extreme. They just loved to talk about Jesus! By the way, that's why they called it the Jesus Movement. In fact, I recall my pastor counseling some radically saved teenagers to stop turning the One Way streets signs in Birmingham in a heavenward direction—that is evandalism, not evangelism!

> Think about it: If someone observed your youth group over time, would they call what was happening there a "Jesus Movement?" If not, what can you do to change that?

Coffeehouses

Countless numbers of teenagers and twentysomethings met Jesus from living on the street. These "street Christians" were among those who started coffeehouse ministries. In 1967 the Hollywood Presbyterian Church opened the Salt Company, a coffeehouse that was the brainchild of college minister Don Williams. The Salt Company affected many people who led in the movement, including Larry Norman, perhaps the very first contemporary Christian musician. Coffeehouses soon began percolating (pardon the pun) across the nation. These began a place where witnessing and counseling occurred, and music appealing to teens was produced. Evenings in the coffeehouses centered on Bible discussions, gospel rock music of some form, and a revival meeting. There are Christian coffeehouses today, but few that intentionally seek to win the unchurched youth to Christ the way they did in the Jesus Movement. Why not start some of those again?

Festivals and rallies also began to emerge. These included large gatherings of people with music, testimonies, and speakers. Contemporary Christian Music began during the early years of the festivals and coffeehouses.

Think about it: What if God began to save some of the gangsters, skinheads, druggies, and homosexuals in your area, while also lighting a fire in the hearts of Christian youth. Just think of what God might do!

An "Explo"sion in '72

Campus Crusade for Christ, the college parachurch ministry, held Explo '72 in Dallas. It resulted in "the most massive gathering of students and Christian laymen to ever descend on one city."[24] Over 80,000 registered for the event, with some 150,000 attending a Saturday music festival concluding the meeting.[25] I had a neighbor who had gotten radically saved while a soldier in Viet Nam. He had returned home, with a very cool bicycle he had purchased in Japan. He rode that bike 700 hundred miles from Alabama to Texas to go to Explo! A former pastor of mine was a youth pastor in 1972. He took over 200 teens from West Palm Beach, Florida, all the way to Dallas on school buses (that's right, no air conditioning). A reporter from a secular newspaper accompanied them, because in 1972 this was big news!

Also, evangelist Billy Graham was very favorable toward what he called the "Jesus Revolution." Aside from writing a book about the movement,[26] Graham noted that during the period he had an unusually high number of youth attending and professing faith in Christ at his crusades.[27]

Asbury College

Probably best known among Evangelicals from this period was the revival at Asbury College of 1970.[28] The revival began somewhat spontaneously during a chapel service on February 3, 1970. The dean of the college was scheduled to speak but felt impressed to have a testimony service. Students began to flood toward the altar to pray. For 185 hours they continuously prayed, sang, and testified. Henry James of the college reported on what happened next:

> Before long, appeals began coming from other campuses for Asbury students to come and tell the story. This intensified the burden of prayer even as it heightened anticipation of what God was going to do, . . .
>
> . . . the revival began to take on the dimensions of a national movement. By the summer of 1970 at least 130 colleges, seminaries and Bible schools had been touched by the revival outreach.[29]

The Asbury revival affected dozens of other schools and scores of churches as students from the college fanned out across the country, telling the story of revival. The revival was marked by serious reflection over personal sin and confession of sins.

Many churches exploded in the 1970s. In fact, many trace the birth of modern megachurches to this period, around 1970. A stirring example in a local church is Houston's First Baptist. John Bisagno came to First Baptist in 1970, when the church was a typical, declining, downtown church. Bisagno kept an eye on the Jesus Movement in California. Unlike many in Southern Baptist circles, Bisagno affirmed the youth of the day. He argued that he would rather see youth "yelling for Jesus that sitting barefoot on a park slope taking drugs."[30] Bisagno led the church to involvement in an effort called SPIRENO (Spiritual REvolution NOw) led by evangelist Richard Hogue. Up to then, no Southern Baptist church had reached as many as one thousand people for Christ in a single year. As a result the church baptized 1,669 for the church year 1970–71, the vast majority coming from young people.[31] One reporter stated: "By taking the initiative, they gave their church and hundreds of others in Houston a chance to jump into the flow of this Jesus Movement."[32] Beyond the evangelistic results cited above, the Jesus Movement helped many traditional churches to focus again on the work of the Holy Spirit. Also, many leaders today in evangelism were converted during or radically touched by the Jesus Movement.[33]

In 2006 and the years following, the largest number of youth in American history will be all around us. What will the church do differently between now and them to reach them? About a year ago I picked up a cassette which featured a collection of songs which debuted in the Jesus Movement. This collection of tunes composed by Larry Norman, called by some the "Poet Laureate of the Jesus Movement," took me back to the early seventies. Only this time, I thought less of disco, rock festivals, and psychedelic drugs, and more of a youth group who radically loved Jesus. Then I thought of a more distant movement, the original Jesus Movement, where a gaggle of Galileans followed the Man we know now to be the Son of God, as recorded in the New Testament. Would you pray for a movement of God to stir your generation for Jesus?

■■■■■■ Excitement made personal

Read Acts 17:1–6 in your Bible. Note in verse 6 where it says of the early believers, "These who have turned the world upside down." Now *that* is excitement! I can remember seeing hippie freaks become Jesus freaks in the early 1970s. They were ready to take on hell with a squirt gun! Ask the Lord to make you more excited about Jesus—about serving Him, about seeing people saved—than anything else.

Chapter Seven

Worship

Enter into His gates with thanksgiving,
and into His courts with praise.
Be thankful to Him and bless His name.
Psalm 100:4

I want to know you,
I want to see your face,
I want to know you Lord.
from the contemporary song
"In the Secret"

DO YOU ENJOY CONTEMPORARY CHRISTIAN MUSIC? IF YOU DO, THANK God for the Jesus Movement. Do you love to sing praise and worship choruses? Ditto. Do you have a contemporary Christian music (CCM) station you listen to? They could not be found before the late 1960s. In no other area has the Jesus Movement made a greater impact than in worship, in the local church, especially in the area of music. Every time in history God has moved in great revival, music in the church changes. The Psalmist understood this, talking about

a new song (See Psalm 33:3). In the 1700s Charles Wesley
wrote over 6,000 hymns, changing the face of music in
England. In the 1970s Scripture, folk music, and pop music came together to form a whole new kind of music that
can be described as simpler and more contemporary than
other music. Some churches struggled with this—the idea
of an electric guitar in some churches was considered to be
a sign of the Antichrist to some (still is, I suppose). I remember when drums entered our sanctuary. Not everyone
was pleased!

The most enduring impact of the Jesus Movement is its
influence on music and worship style. Because of the im-
portance of music in the general youth culture, the role of
music in the Jesus Movement was crucial. The most important impact of the Jesus Movement is not the rise of CCM,
but in the blooming of a wonderful, massive garden of praise
and worship music which is taking a generation of people,
mostly young but also old, to new levels of worship.

A Worship Revolution

In the 1970s most musicians had been so radically saved
they simply sang out of gratitude for Christ. Larry Norman
was one of the best known leaders of Jesus Movement music. His simple ballad about the second coming of Christ,
"I Wish We'd All Been Ready," was a signature song of the
movement. Chuck Girard and his group Love Song were
referred to as the "Beatles of the Christian music world" by
some. Girard continues a musical ministry with the organization Youth with a Mission. Nancy Honeytree met Jesus
Christ in 1970 and soon began to sing in many coffeehouses
and churches her music which blended pop and folk music. Billy Ray Hearn, one of the early leaders in the development of youth musicals, later became an executive with
Sparrow records, and offered Honeytree her first contract.

Don Francisco, son of Southern Baptist Theological Seminary professor Clyde Francisco, was a familiar artist in the early years. Annie Herring became a Christian in 1968 and began singing in California. She formed a group with her sister Nelly and brother Matthew known as the Second Chapter of Acts, a group which remained very popular until they disbanded in 1988.

Barry McGuire epitomized the rock singer-turns-contemporary Christian artist. His protest song "Eve of Destruction" was one of the biggest hits in rock music in 1965. McGuire later had a lead role in the Broadway musical *Hair*. In 1970, McGuire picked up a *Good News for Modern Man* translation of the New Testament. He committed his life to Christ as a result, and traded rock music for the music of the Jesus Movement. Keith Green sang about radical obedience. In 1972 Eddie DeGarmo and Dana Key formed one of the most enduring duos in contemporary Christian music's young history. They were already playing rock music when they began openly singing Christian lyrics. At the time, they knew nothing of Larry Norman or any other Jesus Movement music.

Music plays a major part in the lives of young people in any generation. New music became a natural part of Jesus Movement worship. It was in the less formal setting of coffeehouses and communes where the features of contemporary rock music were easily transferred into Jesus rock music. At The Adam's Apple coffeehouse in Fort Wayne, Indiana several groups began who are still playing. The best known is the Christian rock group Petra. In Nashville the Koinonia coffeehouse was seminal in the rise of CCM. Artists such as Amy Grant, Brown Bannister, and the group Dogwood spent a great deal of time at Koinonia. Likewise, the Jesus festivals provided a forum for musicians to share their songs.

Many of the early CCM singers were rock artists who began singing Christian themes after their conversion. For example, at Calvary Chapel, Costa Mesa, California, four of the members of the pop group Love Song became Christians. They then began singing songs they had written about faith in Christ at Calvary Chapel.

To keep up with the new musical form, the magazine *Contemporary Christian Music* was founded in 1978. A sort of Christian *Billboard* magazine, it included record charts. Don Francisco's "He's Alive" was the first number one song, and the Second Chapter of Acts' "Mansion Builder" was the first top selling album. By 1985, Amy Grant became the first CCM artist to sell one million copies of a single album. The publication has more recently begun a radio countdown (CCM Top 20) and a televised video channel (CCM-TV). In addition, CCM radio stations have continued to be started since the Jesus Movement. Paul Baker was an early leader in this. He was the first to air an "all-Jesus rock radio show" in St. Petersburg, Florida.

The music gave a generation who at times felt left out due to the "generation gap" a spiritual compass. It helped to make the spiritual commitment of the youth more than a Sunday-only experience. As Styll put it, "It's made Christianity relevant for them. . . . Christian music is viable for the other six days of the week, not just Sunday morning."[34]

One of the ways music changed was in the youth musicals. Youth musicals are making a comeback today in many churches. God was at work with teenagers then, and one way He worked was through music. Youth choir tours covered America and Canada, becoming the most effective evangelistic tool of youth groups during that time. For example, in Bridgeport, Connecticut, the 104 voice youth choir from First Baptist, Hendersonville, North Carolina sang twice daily at a week-long "Festival of Faith" crusade.

Some 120 persons made professions of faith. Merchants in the shopping center where the choir sang wrote letters stating that the choir performances "brought a feeling of good cheer in an area where crime had given shoppers [a] sense of uneasiness."[35]

The changes in worship were influenced by young people who came to Christ in the Jesus Movement. The innovations were useful in reaching others as a result.[36] Southern Baptists were in the middle of the dramatic changes taking place. Philip Landgrave commented in 1972 that "in just three years, a dramatic change has taken place in the youth music scene of many congregations."[37] He added that a variety of contemporary expressions, from folk to rock to country and western, had suddenly become acceptable in the worship of traditional and non-traditional churches.

Many coffeehouse ministries featured Jesus rock music written and performed by young people won to Christ out of the rock culture. Similar groups performed at the Jesus festivals. Also, folk youth musicals exploded in number in the late 1960s. Southern Baptists were the major leaders in the early youth musicals, and youth choir tours were more prominent in the early seventies then at any time before or since.

Such musical developments gradually moved into the life of many churches, though not without some consternation on the part of some. Forrest H. Heeren, former dean of the school of music at Southern Seminary, said that musical instruments such as guitars "which ten to fifteen years ago would have been severely questioned are now brought into the regular church service."[38]

The most obvious way one can note the change in music out of the Jesus Movement is by examining the Baptist hymnals of 1975 and 1991. The 1975 *Baptist Hymnal*

Be careful of loving music that is called Christian because it sounds like the music of the world with an occasional reference to God. Contemporary music in itself is not necessarily good or bad; the lyrics make the difference.

included some of the more popular songs of the youth musicals, including "Pass It On" from "Tell It Like It Is" and "Do You Really Care" from "Good News." The newest hymnal demonstrates the continuing effect of the music arising out of the Jesus Movement, for several CCM artists have songs in the hymnal, including Twila Paris and Michael W. Smith.

Worship Changes for Better or Worse

That does not mean all the music was good, or that all CCM today honors Christ. Some did not, and lots of music today does not. In fact, although the early musicians in the Jesus Movement would often drive across the country and sing for no pay, today CCM has become an industry, and the "artists" (formerly known as ministers) too often resemble pop icons in culture than the Lord they claim to serve. In fact, a friend of mine was preaching in a youth meeting with a contemporary band. "You can't talk about God too much when you sing," the band leader said, "It doesn't pay the bills." Today some have forgotten the reason we sing. Sadly, some of the better known musicians, including Amy Grant, Sandy Patty, and Michael English, have brought dishonor to God by immoral behavior. Thankfully, most still sing praises to God with great joy.

CCM began in part as a protest to dead church services which dishonored God by their lack of passion for Him. Like other movements that began as a protest to institutionalism, however, contemporary Christian music itself has become institutionalized, unfortunately. Now a multimillion dollar industry, with its own awards program (the Gospel Music Association's Dove Awards which now has 33 categories) and a category in the Grammies, CCM has established itself as a power in the music industry. From 1980 to 1990, while the overall music industry doubled its revenue, gospel music, in particular contemporary Christian, nearly tripled from $180 million to $500 million. The industry of today looks alarmingly like the establishment the early Christian artists so vehemently opposed.

Part of the reason for the institutionalizing of this music was due to a shift in its development. Contemporary Christian music was primarily evangelistic in its early days. Then, as new record labels were born, Christian radio stations emerged across the country, Christian book and record stores increased, and a concert network began, the audience shifted to Christians primarily. As Styll put it, "Before long, contemporary Christian music had almost totally abandoned its original call to influence popular culture and had become a sub-culture in and of itself."[39]

That attitude was not what gave birth to the music coming out of the Jesus Movement. In the seventies, most simply sought to honor Christ in their music, and to do so in a way that communicated with their peers. Those who continue with that passion are experiencing God in new and incredible ways. Many contemporary Christian record labels still place a premium on the spiritual commitment of its artists. Ron Griffin of Sparrow Records made this point:

"A record contract and a recording are not the point of
your ministry. It only falls in behind the wake of the ministry that God has blessed you with."[40]

The Heart of Worship

Despite the downside of some aspects of CCM, God has
used many of the changes in worship to His glory. You are
part of one of the biggest revolutions in worship ever.
Psalm 40:3 says "He has put a new song in my mouth —
Praise to our God." A whole movement of new hymns
and choruses are energizing youth groups and churches
across the nation.

The chorus to a recent praise and worship song says,
"I'm coming back to the heart of worship, and it's all about
you, all about you Jesus." When worship has that focus—
on the giving ourselves to God—our Lord blesses with His
presence. Across America, in large rooms tucked away
upstairs at local churches, in large arenas, and in CD play-
ers, young people are returning to a fresh, earnest passion
for worship. A recent movement has grown among college students called Passion, which has released several
praise and worship CDs along with a major music festival
with tens of thousands in attendance in May 2000, in Mem-
phis. Of course, there is always the danger in such times
of focusing on the experience of worship over the God we
are called to worship. Still, there is something healthy, even
exciting, about the new wave of worshipers in our day. I
take a team of students in their twenties to help me lead
youth services across the east coast. I am amazed as I watch
young people pour out their hearts to God.

A Generation of Leadership

Beyond music, the greatest impact of the Jesus Movement is still with us. I am referring to a burden for revival. Across the nation, there are leaders in denominations, and in churches, who met God in a powerful way in the early seventies. That explains at least to some degree why so many adults are crying out to God today–many saw a touch of revival, but long to see more. I believe God will take the passion of your generation, and the hunger of mine, and touch our nation in a mighty way. Maybe that is wishful thinking, but I believe!

I am convinced that one of the most effective ways to reach and teach your generation is through praise and worship music combined with biblical, relevant preaching. You and your peers are often called the "millennial" generation, because your high school graduation dates fall after the year 2000. God is moving in some extraordinary ways throughout the fabric of this teen culture. Worship has become a vital part of the Christian young person's experience. It is not uncommon to find teens involved in worship gatherings of up to two hours long. The unrushed atmosphere, spent seeking, and waiting on God, allows these worshipers to heartily confess their sin to God, as well as drink in a sense of His forgiveness, grace, and mercy. Joy and enthusiasm draw young people together.

▬▬▬▬▬▬Worship made personal

Read Psalm 24:1–5. Who is the kind of worshiper God seeks? Someone with clean hands, a pure heart. When you go to public worship on Sunday, or in your youth meetings, do you take time to prepare your heart to encounter God? Here are three practical tips to make worship more meaningful. First, public worship comes from private worship. The more time you spend alone with God, the more real public worship becomes. Second, remember worship is not primarily about you, it is about Him. Keep your focus on Him, and concentrate on honoring Him. Finally, remember this whenever you worship: the more honest you are with God, the more real He will be to you. Open your heart to Him, and experience the mighty presence of God!

Chapter Eight

Obedience

**For me to live is Christ,
and to die is gain.**
Philippians 1:21

**He is no fool
who gives that which he cannot keep,
in order to gain
that which he cannot lose.**
—Jim Elliott

IMAGINE YOU ARE A SAILOR, WITH A GREAT SAILBOAT. YOU CANNOT
control the wind, although you depend on it. You merely
set your sails to move with the wind. In the same way, we
do not force God to send a great revival—however, we can
observe signs, and hoist our sails, so should God move
greatly, we will not be on the shores watching it pass us by
in the distance. Signs indicate the fresh stirring of God's
wind—are you ready?

You are not the first young person to stand at a crucial
crossroads at the turning of a new millennium. Three

millennia ago, a young man stood in the midst of his people, only a youth...

He had no authority as a leader.

He was not a preacher.

He was not well known.

Why, he was not even considered a man—only a boy, a mere youth.

His own family overlooked him, for he was the least in age.

What could this young man do? Why even the man of God, the great prophet Samuel, overlooked this lad. Surely he was too young, good for the next generation, but of no consequence in this. What could he do?

He could stand boldly for his God when others were cowards.

He could fulfill his responsibilities effectively as a shepherd, even when no one watched.

He could take what he had, only a leather strap, a few stones, and what little experience he brought as a shepherd, and give it to his God.

He could demonstrate faith like no one in his nation could, including the very king.

He could stand against Goliath, the most fierce opponent of his day, and win.

He could be a king.

Of all the people on the Bible, no one demonstrates the impact a young person can make more than David. The apostle Paul had an interesting comment about the life of

David in Acts 13:36: "David, after he had served his own generation by the will of God, fell asleep, and was buried with his fathers, . . ." Did you notice that phrase Paul used of David? He *served his own generation*—in other words, when his generation came along, and needed a leader who honored God, David was ready. He stepped up to the plate and hit a grand slam.

The current generation needs an army of David's who will honor God above all else. And, it seems that God is in fact raising up such a generation. David's day was a time of tremendous change, risk, and opportunity. The kingdom had been established, but Saul, the prior king, had not been the leader God had desired. So David, even as a youth, began to refocus the hearts of the people back to God.

David stands as a great example of the fact that one of the most prevalent sayings in the church is dead wrong. How many times have you heard a well-intentioned adult say "youth are the future of the church?" Maybe you have said it. I have, I confess. Okay, so in a sense youth are the future of the church in terms of providing the pastors, missionaries, deacons, teachers, and so on, but my point is this—youth are not *only* the church of the future, you are the hope for the church NOW. David did not have to wait to be an "adult" to serve his generation by the will of God. God's will for him did not begin on his 21st birthday, or his 30th. As a youth, God's hand was already on him.

See, when God measures a person, His primary focus is not on their appearance, or age, or experience, or talent. When God measures you, He puts the tape around your heart (See I Samuel 16:7).

Radical and Fanatical Obedience

What are we to make of the growing violence among young people? Popular culture certainly factors into the escalation of violence. A professor of pediatrics, Vic Strasburger, says, "Clearly the biggest message from movies and TV [might we add video games?] is that violence is an acceptable solution to complex problems."[41] Mike Huckabee, governor of Arkansas and a former Southern Baptist pastor, decried the fact that we live in a culture that breeds such behavior.

In the church, we are quite good at shaking our fist at the dark side of our culture. We call the cultural darkness of our day names. We throw rocks into the darkness of our contemporary ungodliness. But the way to remove darkness is to turn on the Light. None of us as individuals can change society as a whole, but we can change *our* world. We can't touch the life of every troubled youth, but we can influence the life of *some* young person.

Perhaps this wave of youth violence can serve as a wake-up call for the church. In a day in which too many build youth ministry on entertainment, and singles groups on social functions, you can affect a significant part of the youth culture. Instead of trying to out-world the world, why not experience the adventure of a radically-changed life through Christ? Radical, even fanatical, obedience to Jesus is the need of the hour.

Never in American history has your age group been more poised to penetrate the culture than today. The weeks following the disaster in Littleton, Colorado, the Internet, email, Christian clubs, and church youth groups witnessed a surge in spiritual fervor. Since 1990, when the Supreme Court allowed prayer clubs to meet on public school property if they met outside class hours and without adult leadership, many thousands of Bible clubs have exploded across the nation. Most recently this is seen in the rise of a network of First Priority clubs spreading across the nation like a Kansas grass fire.

Teenagers in your generation denote a new breed of evangelical Christians. *Time* magazine reported: "Unlike their evangelical parents, who often defined themselves as outsiders, today's campus Christians, says Barnard College religion professor Randall Balmer, 'Are willing to engage the culture on its terms. They understand what's going on and speak the language.' Teen evangelicals have their own rock concert circuit, complete with stage diving; their own clothing lines, like Witness Wear; and in the omnipresent WWJD ('What Would Jesus Do?') bracelet, their own bracelet accessory.

And now their own martyr."[42]

You hold in your hands the opportunity to impact an entire generation. Get with others and simply seek the face of God. What if, in this generation of students, God sent mighty awakening? What if He touched your youth group? The bottom line is this: God does desire to use you. Pray that God will use the stories of young people in the past to stir today's youth. But first, ask God to send a fresh fire in your heart. Richard Baxter, the Puritan pastor who saw mighty revival in his day, said to leaders: "Your people will know if you have spent much time with God: that will be most in their ears, that is most in your heart."[43] May God give us a heart filled with a passion for Him.

Blow, Spirit, Blow

I mentioned earlier how In September of 1996, our home and others along the eastern seaboard had the ride of our lives. Hurricane Fran hammered the east side of North Carolina like a semi truck over an armadillo. My beautiful Gran Prix had a pine tree down the middle (nothing that about $3,500.00 couldn't fix). We had a hole in our roof, trees down everywhere, and no power for a week. That kind of experience can ruin your whole day! I did learn to cook all kinds of things on a gas grill for a while.

The negative force of a hurricane is a perfect analogy of the positive force of the wind of God's Spirit. Before the hurricane force winds came, there were signs that something was coming. The atmosphere was different, animals acted oddly, one could even catch the scent of the ocean 150 miles from the coast. In the same way, God never sends a mighty revival apart from early signs. What are signs that God is at work today?

*Ten years ago, if someone told you that tens of thousands of men would pay $60.00 apiece to sit for two days in a football stadium to listen to preacher after preacher after preacher, and if they told you that on one day over a million men would come from all across the US to Washington, DC to *repent*, and if they told you that such a thing would happen without a massive, multimillion dollar marketing campaign, you would suddenly have believed in alien life forms. But it has happened in the Promise Keepers movement. And a similar thing is happening among women.

*Maybe you didn't know it, because it is rarely publicized, but did you know that there are thousands and thousands of believers gathering in groups to pray for revival in America? No greater movement of prayer has occurred in our country's existence.

---

*Have you heard anyone talk lately about fasting? When I was in college, I thought fasting went out centuries ago. I thought such practices had gone the way of the dodo, unless you were a monk or something. But now, many have gone on forty day fasts for revival, and unprecedented numbers of believers are learning the discipline of fasting and prayer.

*And of all these, nothing is more encouraging than the wind of the Spirit rustling through students. Note the following:

—*True Love Waits.*

Who would have predicted the marvelous response of youth to the True Love Waits campaign? Hundreds of thousands of teenagers and those in their 20s are signing a covenant, pledging themselves to sexual purity until marriage. Prayerfully dedicated in their church service, many go on to dedicate themselves publicly on their school campuses. These teens are choosing to pursue relationships with the opposite sex in a completely new way. Many, in fact, are "kissing dating good-bye," as a popular seminar by Joshua Harris challenges.[44]

—*See You at the Pole.*

Who suspected that a gathering of teens around a flagpole several years ago would lead to millions joining together annual to "See You at the Pole?" Students gather around their school flagpoles on the third Wednesday of September each year to pray for their schools, communities, friends in need of Christ, and their nation. Begun spontaneously by a church youth group in Dallas, Texas, during a discipleship weekend, SYATP quickly spread to hundreds of churches in the state. The first year, approximately 44,000 teenagers were involved. Three years later, more than 1.5 million kids were reported to have attended. Today there are over three million students and growing who join together at the poles. But SYATP is not just an event. It has initiated students into other courageous and creative ministries. More than 10,000 student-led, on-campus Bible clubs and prayer groups have been started in middle schools, junior highs, and high schools since 1990. Many of these began out of See You at the Pole emphases. And, the tragedy of Wedgwood, which has been used of God to call believers to pray, came during a See You at the Pole Rally on the third Wednesday of September, 1999.

—*Revival on College Campuses.*

On college campuses across America, God is touching students with a fresh breath of revival marked by brokenness and confession of sin. Howard Payne University in Brownwood, Texas, and Wheaton College are two of many examples.

On January 22, 1995, an unusual service at the Coggin Avenue Baptist Church in Brownwood, Texas, became the beginning of a movement of spiritual awakening in that town.[45] College student Chris Robeson exhorted the congregation at the end of the early service that day, after which people began responding in the service in tears and brokenness. The early service extended through the Sunday School hour, past the 11:00 service, into the early afternoon. The spirit of revival quickly spilled over to the nearby campus of Howard Payne University. Coggin Avenue pastor John Avant and many students crisscrossed the nation sharing revival testimonies. Campus after campus and church after church experienced deep brokenness, often including hours of open confession of sin.

Brandi Maguire had no idea when she began her college experience majoring in communication all that God had in store for her. But in the early spring of 1995, Brandi and fellow students at Howard Payne University in Brownwood, Texas, began to see God working in revival. Students began praying together for hours and hours, broken relationships were mended, and lives were radically changed.

Soon Brandi began to go and testify about what God was doing in Brownwood. In Texas, in California, in Illinois, and other states, her testimony sparked repentance and brokenness in the lives of many students. Would you be willing to change your schedule to speak of the mighty acts of God to others?

—Christian clubs.

On public high school campuses across the nation, Christian clubs are starting at an incredible rate. In scores of secondary school across America, students are gathering in their campuses to exercise their faith through prayer and Bible study, find fellowship with other students, and build a platform for sharing Jesus Christ with others. Why is this happening? "Years ago, I discovered that the best way to impact teens on school campuses is through teens on school campuses," says Benny Proffitt, founder and president of First Priority of America.[46]

The 1984 Federal Equal Access Act had opened the door to Christian clubs in secondary schools, provided they were student led and student initiated. Enabling students to "do it themselves" fueled the vision for First Priority. First Priority is centered on campuses, where students spend a majority of their time, but grows out of local church and community support. The strategy includes a citywide youth ministry network, weekly student-led campus club meetings, area-wide ministry

EIGHTH GRADE STUDENT STANDS UP:

This is the first year we have had First Priority at Simpson Middle School. God is blessing us in amazing ways. At the beginning of the school year, 25 to 30 students participated. During the first "Seek Week" of the school year, we had 125 students come to First Priority.

We have a four-week cycle at our meetings called the ACTS Revolution. During the first week we have a time of small group prayer when we pray specifically for certain non-Christians in our school ("A" stands for "accountability"). A guest speaker leads the second week's meeting ("C" stands for a "challenge" from a guest) and then we have prayer time in small groups. The third week is completely student-led ("T" stands for "testimonies and prayer"). Finally, during the fourth week ("S" stands for "Seek Week") we invite all of our non-Christian friends that we have been praying for to join us for First Priority. During this first "Seek Week" of the school year, at the end of the testimony time, 46 students marked on their response card that they had just accepted Christ into their hearts! We are so excited to see God answering our prayers and working in the lives of our friends.

We have had great speakers, teacher sponsors and kids coming to First Priority. We have participated in events such as "See You at the Pole." I hope our numbers will continue to grow and that more people will accept Jesus as their savior. Our prayers during our small groups have a huge impact on our friends, our school and ourselves.

events, and the advocacy of local churches from all denominations, community leaders, business people, parents, and teachers.[47]

Proffitt says that only 20 to 25 percent of teenagers attend church but 95 to 100 percent are in school five days a week. First Priority "Great Commission" clubs enable students to reach these unchurched young people and then offer follow-up and nurture through participating churches. The clubs also unite Christian students on their campuses, providing positive peer pressure and accountability to one another. By 1999 First Priority was active in 175 cities nationwide and had trained teens for student-led ministry in more than 3,000 schools.

That First Priority is seizing the day for effective ministry among youth is reflected in the comment of a ninth grader from Atlanta, Georgia: "I used to think it was wrong to bring a Bible to school. . . . I [felt] totally alone as a Christian. Now I know I am surrounded by friends who are also excited about sharing our faith with others." A similar emphasis called "Fishing the Planet" has been initiated by the North American Mission Board of the Southern Baptist Convention.

Christian clubs touch the lives of millions. Surely God is up to something. Are we ready?

—An Army of the Obedient.

The brightest sign on the spiritual horizon is the growing zeal of multitudes of students, people just like you. Sadly, this comes often in stark contrast to so many active, adult, middle aged church members who seem satisfied to be sanctified. Oh, that God would give us all a fresh fire for Him!

Gene Edward Veith recently observed the positive side of the youth culture. He sadly but accurately mentioned the problems of young people today, but also he accurately put the blame where much of it lies—with parents, the "aging baby boomers who continue to vandalize the civilization, refusing to be parents, rejecting moral and intellectual absolutes, manufacturing a decadent popular culture and making lots of money by selling it to children."[48]

Such behavior has produced numerous casualties among young people. But Veith gives the positive side:

> But there are signs that this next generation is engaged in another rebellion—this time a healthy one—against the status quo.
>
> The postmodernist establishment of the adult world celebrates superficiality. Since in this worldview there is no truth, everything is make-believe. This leaves some in the next generation craving authenticity. *They want something honest. They want something real.*[49]

Veith cited evidence for the change in your generation. A survey of college freshmen since 1966 by the Higher Education Research Institute at the University of California-Los Angeles discovered in 1998 the lowest support ever recorded for casual sex. Whereas in 1987, 52 percent, or over half believed casual sex was acceptable, the latest survey found only 40 percent in favor. Also, in 1998 the lowest number ever favored abortion.

Are similar changes going on elsewhere? If so, there's reason to be optimistic about this new generation. Obedience to God seems to be a choice your peers want to make.

▋▋▋▋▋ Obedience made personal

Read I Samuel 17:17–25. Notice what Samuel said to king Saul: "To obey is better than sacrifice." A lot of Christianity is simply deciding to obey God. God is calling you to radical obedience. He may lead you to surrender your entire life in some form of vocational ministry. He may even give you the wonderful privilege of spending your life overseas as a missionary. Regardless of your specific assignment, He is worthy of your supreme surrender.

Stop for just a moment and imagine. Suppose the Spirit of God began to move deeply in your youth group, or singles fellowship, or on your college campus. It would not be the first time, but there has likely never been a time in American history that revival was needed more. What if God really were beginning to stir His church in a way unlike that which we have seen in decades, if not generations? Guess what? Whether we will see great revival, we *can* see the hand of God working in incredible ways in each of our lives–yes, that includes you! If God *does* this, He will look for someone just like you to join Him. Let's set the sails!

Chapter Nine

Prayer

Call to Me, and I will answer you,
and show you great and mighty things,
which you do not know.

Jeremiah 33:3

The only time you will find power before prayer
is in the dictionary.

Comment from an elderly believer
to me as a young preacher

IN SEPTEMBER, 2000, I SPOKE AT A CHURCH JUST WEST OF ASHEVILLE, NC. That afternoon I went out witnessing with some church members. One of them commented that she had gone to a "We Still Pray" rally in Asheville just weeks before. "Well," she said, "I never made it to the rally. Three of us sat in traffic, but one person I know made it in." One newspaper estimated that *thirty-five thousand* came to the rally on August 17 to protest the Supreme Court's ruling in June about school prayer at ball games. As a result, "We Still Pray" rallies have sprung up across the nation. Christians have

been encouraged, and across America many have, to spontaneously speak the Lord's Prayer after the national anthem
at ball games.[49]

This same September of 2000, approximately three million students gathered at their schools' flag poles for the sev-
enth annual See You at the Pole prayer event, perhaps the
largest simultaneous prayer meeting in American history. See
You at the Pole has sparked a nationwide interest in prayer
among teens.[50]

> When God begins to work, he gets His people praying.
>
> —Matthew Henry

An Awesome Way to Pray

"I consider myself one of the biggest supporters of See You
at the Pole," says Barry St. Clair, founder of Reach Out Ministries, a youth ministry training organization in Atlanta.
"But I wondered, 'How can we take this thing from a one-
day event to a national movement among our young
people?'" Pursuing this question with much prayer and dili-
gent effort, Reach Out Ministries developed the Pole2Locker
concept, now called An Awesome Way to Pray.

An Awesome Way to Pray is "designed to help young
people take their commitment for Christ, demonstrated at
the See You at the Pole event, to their lockers – that is, to
their spheres of influence in their schools." says St. Clair.
An Awesome Way to Pray is a six-week intensive training
course designed to help today's teens reach their peers with
the gospel. It focuses teens on three main things: loving
their friends, living the life, and telling the story. "When
we as leaders demonstrate genuine concern for young
people and equip them to live out their faith, we energize

them for the work of the kingdom," says St. Clair. "They are changed—and so are we."[51]

Lead, Join, or Get out of the Way

High school students in Modesto, California, are doing Jericho-style prayerwalks around every school in their city. Mike Higgs reported in *Pray!* Magazine that in places like Littleton, Colorado, students began establishing a prayer groups on every campus in their community. Notice: His article highlighted Littleton, Colorado, in an issue which was published just months *before* the tragedy of Columbine. He noted prior to the Columbine tragedy there was a vision for seeing campus prayer groups established throughout metropolitan Denver and across the nation. Young people from Portland, Oregon, to Buffalo, New York, are engaging in protracted times of united prayer literally crying out to God for their peers, schools, and communities.[52]

Higgs commented:

> There seems to be an unprecedented, unplanned, unusual, and unstoppable explosion of prayer among youth! It's unprecedented, at least in modern times, because of the sheer number of participants. It's unplanned because it's not the result of some new youth ministry program or activity. It appears to be a quite spontaneous work of the Holy Spirit, and nobody is trying to control it. It's unusual because such passion for prayer is not what's expected from a postmodern, relativistic, universalism-embracing culture. And it's unstoppable because it can't be legislated out of the schools—you can take *prayer* out of schools, but you can't take the *praying students* out![53]

Recent articles in *Time* magazine, the *Washington Post,* and other publications, as well as a special report on CNN, have brought national attention to this grass-roots movement. So did the recent shooting tragedy involving victims

When faced with a busy day, save time by skipping your devotional time.

Signed, The DEVIL

from a school prayer group in Paducah, Kentucky. But media publicity only touches the tip of the iceberg. During a series of national youth leader meetings surrounding the National Day of Prayer gathering in Washington, D.C., testimony after testimony of how God is stirring up prayer in youth circulated through the groups.

More and more, phrases such as "moral wilderness" and "desert wasteland" are being used to describe our cultural terrain. Some people borrow the biblical terms "dry bones" and "desolation" to note the increasing depravity, loss of personal integrity, and idolatry of the 1990s. Even within the church, many point to the absence of a distinctively Christian character. But as we survey today's desolate society, some signs of hope and new life can be spotted on the horizon—in the vibrancy and passion of Christian youth. These young people may be the precursors to one of the greatest moves of God's Spirit we've seen.

Revival and the Power of Prayer

Revival is a lifestyle of obedience to God. Such a lifestyle is born out of a life of prayer. I define prayer this way: *Intimacy with God that leads to the fulfillment of His purposes.* It involves *intimacy*, which is more than just talking. Prayer paves the road to a close, daily, personal walk with our Lord. It leads to the fulfillment of *His* purposes. Prayer is not a Santa Claus-like wish list; it is our way to learn God's purposes for us. Remember, life is not primarily about us, but about Him.

Let me offer a few practical tips to help you have a daily, close walk with God. If you do not have a time set aside daily to spend with Jesus, think about this: you take time daily to eat, to sleep, and (I *hope*) to clean up. Surely God is worth some of our time as well. You will never go further as a Christian than your time with God.

As you set aside time daily, start by reading the Bible. If you do not know where to begin, you might try reading a chapter of Proverbs each day, reading a chapter that goes with the day of the month (Proverbs 1 for May 1, for example). Ask your youth pastor or another leader for help in this also. Then, spend some time talking to God. Keeping a spiritual journal helps. I have kept one for many years. I like to write a little about the day before (I usually start out with "Yesterday I . . ."). Then, I will share my requests, and sometimes my plans.

When praying try following the little guide ACTS:

A is for Adoration
Spend some time praising God for His greatness. Sometimes you might listen to a praise and worship song as a part of this time.

C is for Confession
Ask God to reveal any sins and confess those (I John 1:9).

T is for Thanksgiving
Growing Christians are grateful Christians. Thank God for salvation, and for His specific blessings.

S is for Supplication
This is a big word meaning to ask God for your needs and for the needs of others. I like to keep a list of specific things for which I am praying. Then, when God answers, I write that down, which really encourages me!

Here are a few very practical things you can do to help with maintaining a daily devotional time:[54]

1. Make your devotional time a priority.
I am sure you have a busy life–we all do! But you have time to do what you believe to be important. Set aside a time to spend with God, and stick to it as much as possible. Remember, sometimes you won't *feel* like praying, but you should pray because it is right, not because of your emotions.

2. Designate a set time and place for your time with God.
Guard the time. For me it is first thing in the morning. Find a time best for you.

3. Do whatever is necessary to be spiritually prepared.
Take a shower, listen to a song, or cut on some lights. I need a fresh cup of coffee!

4. Adjust your time occasionally to avoid monotony.
Sometimes I pray first, then read God's Word, sometimes I reverse that, and so on.

5. As you pray, make the Scriptures a part of your time.
A great saint of prayer from years ago said: "We can do more than pray after we pray than pray, but we cannot do more than pray until we pray."

Your Generation Holds the Key

Teens have discovered that a revived life is not based on wishful thinking or emotional exuberance. Those who are on the road of revival are there because they know they have been purchased, rescued, and ransomed by a gracious God. This leads to gratitude, worship, and inner joy. Most young people who choose to confess their sin and devote themselves to Christ are keenly aware of the ravages of sin in their lives and in our culture. It is against this backdrop that God seems to be moving teenagers into a new frontier. In virtually every region of the country, revival passion among young people has formed a spring that is slowly but surely gushing into the cultural desert.

I believe your generation has more promise for a genuine, God-inspired revival than any in a long time. Your own opinions help to support this.

The "Millennials" (coined by author and generation cycles-watcher William Strauss) have the following observations made of yourselves:

- You are optimistic about God's ability to impact the future.

- You are keenly aware of the culture's hypocrisy and moral conflicts.

- You see through the superficiality of God's people.

- You recognize the duplicity and injustice in our culture's values.

- You are open to new and better ways.

- You are easily energized and mobilized for action.

- You are willing to take risks.

- You are often courageous and will stand alone against the status quo.

- You are passionate about a cause that will capture your imagination.[55]

God has a heart for the young. Biblical history, as well as church history, reveals that when God moves in dramatic ways, young people are often at the center of the movement or the ones most greatly affected. The traits of youth-ful believers should give us hope—and perspective—for today and the future. Let God take your passion and turn it into a life of prayer.

Prayer made personal

Read Mark 1:35. Even the Lord Jesus spent much time in prayer. How much more do we need to spend time with God? If you ever get frustrated with prayer, maybe you need to remember this little reminder of how God often works in prayer:

When you ask God something,

- Sometimes God says *no* because the *request* is wrong (we sometimes ask for things that God knows will hurt us)
- Sometimes God says *slow* because the *timing* is wrong (God is never early or late, but sometimes we are impatient)
- Sometimes God says *grow* because *you* are wrong (sometimes we are just not spiritually mature enough yet)
- BUT, when the request is right, and the time is right, and you are right, God says GO!

Chapter Ten

Honesty

Blessed are the undefiled in the way,
who walk in the way of the Lord!
Blessed are those who keep His testimonies,
Who seek Him with the whole heart!
—David, in Psalm 119:1-2

You know, I wonder what God is going to do with my life.
Like my purpose.
Some people become missionaries and things,
but what about me?
What does God have in store for me?
Where do my talents and gifts lie?
For now, I'll just take it day by day.
I'm confident that I'll know someday.
Maybe I'll look back at my life and think, 'Oh, so that was
it!' Isn't it amazing, this plan we're a part of? . . .
—Cassie Bernall,
in a letter to her friend Cassandra, 6-28-98[56]

DENVER, COLORADO. WHAT A GORGEOUS CITY. BASKING IN THE glow of back to back Super Bowl Championships by their beloved Broncos, Denver stood ready to move into the new millennium. I visited the Mile High City on April 10–11, 1999. The sun shined brightly. People I met seemed upbeat.

Then, two weeks later, the gunshots sounded. Bombs exploded. A pastor friend who came to Columbine the day of the disaster said it looked like a war zone. How could this be? Two high school students attacked their peers, leaving fifteen death that day, including themselves. The Columbine tragedy followed others, but this one seemed to capture the attention of the nation like few events in recent years.

As the news came out concerning the tragedy, several names stood out as heroic. One of these was Cassie Bernall. An attractive 17-year old, Cassie died because she had the audacity to admit she believed in Jesus Christ. Rachel Scott also died for her faith. Now Cassie and Rachel are like Abel from the Bible—though dead, they live. Her life, epitomized in her death as a martyr, powerfully demonstrates the impact a teenager can have on a nation. The slaughter of innocent students at Columbine High School in April, 1999, has touched the soul of America. Unfortunately, such madness is no longer unusual:[57]

- October 1, 1997: A sixteen-year old boy is arrested for allegedly killing his mother, then shooting nine students at his high school, killing two. Some evidence points to a conspiracy with a group who dabbled in Satanism.

- December 1, 1997: A fourteen-year old is arrested and charged with opening fire on a student prayer circle in West Paducah, Kentucky, killing three and wounding five.

- December 15, 1997: A boy, age fourteen, is charged with wounding two students with sniper fire in Stamps, Arkansas.

These are only a few of the many acts of violence in our culture among youth.

Hope out of Despair

Students are accustomed to taking tests. That goes with the territory of being a student. You LOVE tests, don't you? Okay, maybe not. Truth is, you may have taken some bad exams in your time, but some students at Columbine High School in Littleton, Colorado, took the ultimate test in April of 1999. A gunman, a fellow student, not a Middle Eastern terrorist, but a fellow classmate, asked the question, "Do you believe in God?" And because two students passed the test, they were shot to death. Cassie Bernall and Rachel Scott met with a horrific and early death because of the test they faced.

For her funeral, friends of Cassie Bernall prepared a video, which included their memories with photographs of the young woman with long blond hair and a radiant smile. "Her eyes shone with Christ's light," one of the friends said in the video. "Cassie was one of the strongest Christians I've ever known," said another friend. "I knew that she was so willing to die for Christ." Added a third: "I just thank God she went out . . . a martyr. She went out dying for what she believed."

Amazingly the deaths of Cassie and Rachel, rather than diminishing the commitment of Christian youth in an increasingly secular society, have served as a rallying point. In sermons and youth groups and quiet moments of personal reflection, these students [killed for their faith at

---

This was found in a New York Newspaper:

Dear God,
Why didn't you save the students in the Littleton Schools?
Sincerely
Student

Answer:

Dear Student,
I'm not allowed in schools.
Sincerely
God

Columbine] are being heralded in saintlike terms. For some teenagers and adults, the deaths are strengthening individual belief. For others, the senseless violence has evoked a specter of religious persecution. Such interpretation is not surprising. For one thing, the tragedy of Columbine took its greatest toll on teenagers. In addition, it took place at a time when Christianity, especially in its evangelical form, is attracting increasing interest among adolescents and young adults across the country.[58]

After the tragedy CNN aired the funeral for the victims of Columbine and through this one airing alone thousands accepted Christ as Savior! Also, it was during this funeral service that pastor Bruce Porter spoke and asked all in attendance and those watching by television, "Who among you young people will pick up the torch that Rachel has dropped?" Out of the 3,000 in attendance 1,000 stood to their feet. It has been reported that literally all across the country, young people who were watching the funeral, heard Mr. Porter's challenge and stood in response wherever they were at that moment. The gunmen that day, Eric Harris

and Dylan Klebold, assaulted students and then killed themselves, ironically with the same kind of prejudice that drove
them to their ungodly acts. They were targeted by some, in
particular athletes, for ridicule and abuse. Never would this
excuse their acts, and certainly it does not excuse their own
practice of seeking out those with whom they disagreed as

A COLUMBINE STUDENT WROTE:

The paradox of our time in history is that we have taller buildings, but
shorter tempers; wider freeways, but narrower viewpoints; we spend
more, but have less; we buy more, but enjoy it less. We have bigger
houses and smaller families; more conveniences, but less time; we have
more degrees, but less sense; more knowledge, but less judgment;
more experts, but more problems; more medicine, but less wellness.

We have multiplied our possessions, but reduced our values. We
talk too much, love too seldom, and hate too often. We've learned
how to make a living, but not a life; we've added years to life, not life
to years. We've been all the way to the moon and back, but have
trouble crossing the street to meet the new neighbor. We've conquered
outer space, but not inner space; we've cleaned up the air, but polluted
the soul; we've split the atom, but not our prejudice. We have higher
incomes, but lower morals; we've become long on quantity, but short
on quality. These are the times of tall men, and short character; steep
profits, and shallow relationships.

These are the times of world peace, but domestic warfare; more
leisure, but less fun; more kinds of food, but less nutrition. These are
the days of two incomes, but more divorce; of fancier houses, but
broken homes.

It is time when there is much in the show window and nothing in
the stockroom; a time when technology can bring this letter to you, and
**a time when you can choose either to make a difference. . . or just
hit delete.**

the targets of their venom. Jocks, minorities, and yes, Christians were targeted that day. According to some accounts eight of the thirteen young people killed that day claimed the Christian faith.

Cassie's Story

Ironically, Cassie Bernall only two years earlier found herself heading down a path similar to that of Klebold and Harris. She began hanging with the wrong crowd, and in particular a young lady who wrote Cassie letters which spewed profanity and featured grisly themes. Cassie's friend would depict herself in the letters as a vampire monkey wearing a pentagram necklace. So many teens today are obsessed with the darker side of reality, from vampires, to death, to occultism. Cassie was being sucked into this quicksand of negativity, to the point that in her mind she sold her soul to the devil. By the way, you can't really do that!

One day, Cassie's mom discovered a stack of these letters. Shocked and amazed, she and her husband confronted Cassie. Ultimately, they moved her to a private school, refused to let her see her old friends, and did everything they could to turn her life in another direction. Was Cassie happy? No, not at all. At least not at first. In fact, she tried secretly to stay in contact with her former friends, even planning to sneak out to go to a Marilyn Manson concert. Even her youth pastor thought she was beyond reach: "I told them they were welcome to bring Cassie to our youth group activities, and that we'd do our best to help her, but underneath I never gave Cassie a hope. I remember walking away from that meeting and saying to myself, "We'll give it our best, but this girl's going to be a hard one. She's gone, unreachable. There is no way that she'll ever recover from what she's doing."[59] Until the day she went on a retreat.

P.S. Honestly, I want to live completely for God. It's hard and scary, but totally worth it.

—Note written by Cassie the night before her death, handed to her friend Amanda the next AM at school.[63]

A friend at her private school invited her to the retreat. The friend, Jamie, remembered what happened:

There was a nighttime praise-and-worship service. I don't remember what the guy talked about, though the theme of the weekend was overcoming the temptations of evil and breaking out of the selfish life. It was the singing that for some reason just broke down Cassie's walls. It really seemed to change her. I wasn't expecting much out of the whole thing, also not for her, because she'd always been so closed. I thought: just one weekend is not going to change her, though it could help. So when she totally broke down, I was pretty shocked.

Actually we were outside the building, and Cassie was crying. She was pouring out her heart–I think she was praying–and asking God for forgiveness. Inside a lot of kids had been bringing stuff up to the altar–drug paraphernalia and stuff like that; they were breaking off their old bonds.[60]

Jamie commented on the change in perspective the night brought, as the two girls and a few others went to the top of a mountain and gazed at the greatness of God. "We just stood there in silence for several minutes, totally in awe of God. It was phenomenal: our smallness, and the bigness of the sky. The bigness of God was so real," Jamie recalled. "Later I noticed that Cassie's whole face had changed. . . . it was like her eyes were more hopeful. There was something new about her."[61]

Cassie's Mom Misty recalled the change in her daughter: "I'm not sure she even knew what all this religious stuff meant–you know, people asking her about being born again or saved or whatever. But she did know that she had found something that was going to fulfill her in a way that nothing else had up till then, and if I think about it, the thing that showed up most was her smile. She began to smile."[62]

Chuck Colson observed that Cassie Bernall's favorite movie was "Braveheart," in which the hero dies a martyr's death.[64] A 17-year-old junior, Cassie had talked of cutting off her long blond hair to have it made into wigs for cancer patients who had lost their hair through chemotherapy.

Thinking of the death of Cassie, I recall how as a youth I carried a Bible to school, as Cassie did. It never occurred to me in my high school days that someone who carried a Bible might die, perhaps for being so open about her faith.

According to Colson, Cassie was in the library reading her Bible when the two young killers barged in the room. An eyewitness and close friend named Mickie Cain told CNN host Larry King: "When the killers asked her if there was anyone who had faith in Christ. She spoke up and they shot her for it." After her open confession of belief in Christ, the killer reportedly asked, "Why?" and shot her.

Honesty and Reality

Why *would* a young lady answer the way she did, knowing her life was in danger? Why should you serve Jesus, after

All of us should live life so as to be able to face eternity at any time.
—Underlined sentence in a devotional book read by Cassie Bernall.

all? Because Mom and Dad said it is right? Because your pastor or student minister told you that you'd better speak up for Jesus? Think about it, if you were facing the bottom of a gun barrel, why should you confess Christ?

Why? Because Jesus left heaven to face the nasty spikes of a Roman cross. Because Jesus did more than die, He died with the weight of the world's sins. Because He has a home in heaven for you that you don't deserve. Because He is coming back and you should be ready. All of these and more are reasons.

But let me just be practical. You need to be ready to confess Jesus even at the point of death, because of this simple reason: *until you are ready to die, you aren't really living.* Cassie and Rachel, and some of their peers, had learned to live by being ready to die.

For Cassie, and others like her, God was not a concept that you claim belief in when you go to church or when you are around religious people. God was as real to her as the air she breathed. Read this statement carefully: When you become *honest* with God, He will become *real* to you. Is God real to you? Are you completely, totally honest to Him?

Cassie's friend Mickie Cain told Larry King that Cassie was "fun loving and amazingly open hearted, and—you could come to her with anything." The glow of God shined from her face. Cassie's God is real–is He real to you?

A student at Southeastern Seminary recently told me the name of his new baby girl–Cassandra. She goes by the name Cassie–as in Cassie Bernall. His prayer is that God will raise a generation of young people with her passion.

Tragedy of tragedies, young people dying a martyr's death. But look closer. When Cassie met her untimely fate, she was walking so close to Jesus, the step from this life to the life beyond was a short one. What about you? Do you walk with Jesus so closely, that if your life were cut short for any reason, the change from here to heaven would be a simple one?

▬▬▬ Honesty made personal

Consider some of the last written words of Cassie Bernall:

According to the Boston Globe, on the night of her death, Cassie's brother Chris found where Cassie had written the words of Philippians 2 from the *Living Bible*. She had written these words just two days prior to her death. It read:

> Now I have given up on everything else
> I have found it to be the only way
> To really know Christ and to experience
> The mighty power that brought
> Him back to life again, and to find
> Out what it means to suffer and to
> Die with him. So, whatever it takes
> I will be one who lives in the fresh
> Newness of life of those who are
> *Alive from the dead.*"

Are you willing to die for Jesus? Honestly? Perhaps a more real question is this: Are you willing to *live* for Jesus?

————— Conclusion

As an evangelist, Rodney "Gypsey" Smith preached in England and America. This evangelist saw God move mightily in great revival. Once someone asked Gypsey Smith how to experience personal revival.

"If you want a revival," Smith said, "Go home, and draw a chalk line round yourself, and stand in the ring and say 'Lord, begin here!'"[65]

To you, the reader, regardless of your age, I have one simple message: it is chalk time. Will you search your heart, not the heart of your youth group, or your parents, but your heart?

Another evangelist from years ago said this: If you want to see God work mightily in your life, do three things.

First, let a small group of Christians get totally right with God. This book has been a call for you to do just that.

Second, let that group put themselves totally at God's disposal, so He can use them for His purposes.

Third, let them bind together for prayer. Would you, and a few others do this? God can use you, if you will let Him.

Let God light the fire of His presence in your life.

Revival

I'm getting tired of my excuses
I know You must be tired as well
but I'm getting ready for some changes I can tell
maybe I should give up the whole thing
just make believe that I am dead
but I hear You screaming resurrection in my head
for far too long
I've been not so strong
there are times I feel barely alive
but I think its time that I revive

Sometimes the people make me angry
sometimes the pictures make me stare
there are times the world is so in need and I don't care
sometimes my brokenness is tragic
other times it opens up my eyes
sometimes it comes along and knocks me down to size
thought I'd done my best for you
and more or less that's true
but to live is not to simply survive
I think its time that I revive

One cry/ one prayer
You roll the stone away
I know You're waiting
Your life in me can lift me from my grave
 one cry/ one prayer
and I'm no longer there

I've got a problem with receiving
I know You've done the best You can
but somehow I never seem to open up my hands
You've been my master and my savior
but I've not been Your slave
Your servant, Your soldier, Your disciple
I need Your revival[66]

Endnotes

1. Words and music by Brian Doerksen and Bob Baker. Used by permission.

2. See Malcolm McDow and Alvin L. Reid, *Firefall: How God Has Shaped History Through Revivals* (Nashville: Broadman and Holman, 1997); J. Edwin Orr, *Campus Aflame* (Wheaton: International Awakening Press).

3. Jonathan Edwards, "A Faithful Narrative of the Surprising Work of God, in the Conversion of Many Hundred Souls, in Northampton, and the Neighbouring Towns and Villages of New Hampshire, in New England; in a Letter to the Rev. Dr. Colman, of Boston," In *The Works of Jonathan Edwards*, ed. Sereno E. Dwight (London: Banner of Truth Trust, 1834), Vol. I, 347.

4. Jonathan Edwards, "Some Thoughts Concerning the Present Revival of Religion in New England, and the Way in Which It Ought to Be Acknowledged and Promoted, Humbly Offered to the Public, in a Treatise on That Subject," in *The Works of Jonathan Edwards*, I:423.

5. Taken from Lynn Vincent, "Gunpoint Evangelist," *World* October 9, 1999, 16–19.

6. Elisabeth Elliott, *Through Gates of Splendor* (Wheaton: Tyndale, 1981), 18.

7. Elisabeth Elliot. *Shadow of the Almighty* (San Francisco: Harper, 1989), 76.

8. Ibid., 104.

9. Excerpts taken from *Shadow of the Almighty*.

10. J. Edwin Orr, *Flaming Tongue* (Chicago: Moody Press, 1973), 3.

11. Ibid., 5.

12. James A. Stewart, *Invasion of Wales by the Spirit though Evan Roberts* (Ft. Washington, PA: Christian Literature Crusade, 1970), 28–29.

13. Arnold Dallimore, *George Whitefield* (Edinburgh: Banner of Truth, 1970), I:73.

14. McDow and Reid, *Firefall,* 189.

15. Alvin Reid, *Introduction to Evangelism* (Nashville: Broadman and Holman,1998), 51.

16. McDow and Reid, *Firefall*, 189.

17. Evan Roberts, in W.T. Stead, ed., *The Story of the Welsh Revival* (London: Fleming H. Revell, 1905), 6.

18. Jonathan Edwards, ed. "The Life and Diary of the Rev. David Brainerd," in *Complete Works*, II:347.

19. "The Crosses of Columbine High School." Darrell Scott speaking at First Baptist Church Springdale, Arkansas. September 5, 1999.

20. McDow and Reid, *Firefall*, 229.

21. See Chauncy A. Goodrich, "Narrative of Revivals of Religion in Yale College," *American Quarterly Register* 10 (Feb. 1838): 295–96.

22. Brian Edwards, *Revival* (Edinburgh: Banner of Truth, 1990), 53.

23. See Alvin L. Reid, "The Effects of the Jesus Movement on Evangelism among Southern Baptists," Ph.D. Dissertation, Southwestern Baptist Theological Seminary, 1991.

24. "Baptists among 80,000 attending Explo '72," *Indiana Baptist*, 5 July 1972, 5.

25. Ibid.

26. Billy Graham, *The Jesus Revolution* (Grand Rapids: Zondervan, 1971).

27. David Kucharsky, "Graham in Gotham," *Christianity Today*, 17 July 1970, 30; "Overflow Crowds of Youth Attend Graham Crusade," *Indiana Baptist*, 12 May 1971, 7.

28. Robert Coleman was on the faculty at that time and edited a history of the revival entitled *One Divine Moment* (Old Tappan, NJ: Fleming H. Revell, 1970).

29. Henry C. James, "Campus Demonstrations," in *One Divine Moment*, 55.

30. Dallas Lee, "The Electric Revival," *Home Missions* June/July 1971, 33.

31. "Tex. Baptist Church Sets New SBC Baptism Record," *Indiana Baptist*, 15 December 1971, 5. The highest number the year before was only 395.

32. Lee, "Electric Revival," 34.

33. There are too many to name, but some examples of those who were touched by or provided leadership to the Jesus Movement were evangelist Jay Strack, Ohio Evangelism Director Mike Landry, HMB Evangelism Section staffer Jack Smith, Glenn Sheppard, who became the first to lead the Office of Prayer and Spiritual Awakening at the HMB, and many others. This writer, whose dissertation was on the Jesus Movement, was amazed to discover how many people today testify to the enduring positive impact on their lives.

34. Tim Stafford, "Has Christian Rock Lost Its Soul?" *Christianity Today* November 22, 1993, 19.

35. "Conn. 'Festival of Faith' Results in 120 Decisions," *Indiana Baptist* 12 July 1972, 5.

36. Donald Hustad of Southern Seminary stated that "It should be obvious that the motivation behind all the pop-gospel phenomena of our day is evangelism...." In "Music in the Outreach of the Church," (Southern Baptist Church Music Conference, 9–10 June 1969), p. 48.

37. Philip Landgrave, "Church Music and the 'Now Generation,'" *Review and Expositor* LXIX (Spring 1972): 195.

38. Forrest H. Heeren, "Church Music and Changing Worship Patterns," *Review and Expositor* LXIX (Spring 1972): 190.

39. John W. Styll, "Sound and Vision: 15 Years of Music and Ministry," *Contemporary Christian Music* (July 1993), 43.

40. "How to Get Signed in the '90s—Part 2," *Contemporary Christian Music* July 1993, 24.

41. Karen S. Peterson and Glenn O'Neal, "Society More Violent; So Are Its Children," *USA Today* (March 25, 1998), 3A.

42. Nancy Gibbs, "In Sorrow and Disbelief," *Time*, May 3 1999, 58.

43. McDow and Reid, *Firefall*, 172.

44. Lani Hinkle, *Pray!*, Sept/Oct. 1998, 14.

45. Ibid.

46. Ibid.

47. Gene Edward Veith, "In praise of teenagers," *World*, May 15 1999, 34.

48. Ibid., emphasis added.

49. Art Toalston, "'We Still Pray' Aims to Go National with Rallies, Prayer at Football Games," Baptist Press Release, August 22, 2000.

50. Lani Hinkle, *Pray!*, Sept/Oct. 1998, 22.

51. Ibid. An Awesome Way to Pray resources are available from Lifeway Christian Resources. For more information or to order, call (800) 458-2772.

52. Higgs, *Pray!*, 18. "Go for it" attitude ignites a prayer explosion among teens.

53. Ibid., 19.

54. These are adapted from my book *Introduction to Evangelism*, 144–45.

55. Ibid., 16. Doug Tegner is the national coordinator for the Challenge 2000 Alliance. For more information on Challenge 2000 call (619) 615-8480 or go on-line to www.challenge2000.org.

56. Misty Bernall. *She Said Yes: The Unlikely Martyrdom of Cassie Bernall*. (Farmington, PA: The Plough Publishing House, 1999), 99–100

57. Taken from "Schools Hit by Violence," *USA Today* (March 25, 1998), 3A.

58. Ibid., A03.

59. Bernall, *She Said Yes*, 52.

60. Ibid., 81–82.

61. Ibid., 82.

62. Ibid., 92–93.

63. Ibid., ix.

64. Charles W. Colson, "Littleton's Martyrs," BreakPoint Commentary, April 26, 1999.

65. Smith, Gipsy, *The Beauty of Jesus: Memories and Reflections* (London: Epworth Press, 1932). 169.

66. Words and music by Ross Sullivan King and Kevin Smith. Copyright 1999 Ross King/Kevin Smith from the album "Big Quiet Truth". Note: Ross writes, "It's time for us to live like resurrected warriors. . . One cry, one prayer..."

To order additional copies of

Light the Fire

Have your credit card ready and call

toll free **(877) 421-READ (7323)**

or send $9.99 each plus $4.95 S&H*

to

**WinePress Publishing
PO Box 428
Enumclaw, WA 98022**

www.winepresspub.com

*WA residents, add 8.6% sales tax

* Add $1.00 S&H for each additional book ordered.